A Girl's Guide to Retail Therapy

Unleash the Healing Power of Shopping

AMY ELLIOTT

ILLUSTRATIONS BY ROBIN ZINGONE

BARNES & NOBLE

NEW YORK

 A QUIRK PACKAGING BOOK
Edited by Sarah Scheffel
Designed by Lynne Yeamans

2006 Barnes & Noble Publishing

ISBN-13: 978-0-7607-8355-9
ISBN-10: 0-7607-8355-1

Printed and bound in China

1 3 5 7 9 10 8 6 4 2

WARNING: Retail therapy only works if you know your limits, as spending beyond
your means can wreak havoc on your finances, relationships, and even your sanity.
While this book suggests many modes of shopping to ease your troubles, it does
not condone compulsive shopping—that is a chronic, uncontrollable pattern of
purchasing things you don't need and/or can't afford. If you suffer from compulsive
shopping and spending, you don't need retail therapy, you need real therapy.
Help for shopping addiction is also available at the National Foundation for Credit
Counseling (debtadvice.org) or Debtors Anonymous (debtorsanonymous.org).

For my mother

Contents

What is retail therapy? It's shopping to make yourself feel better fast, whether you're depressed, lovelorn, bored, blue, or just looking for cheap thrills. The term is often used flippantly ("Jane? No, she's not on antidepressants, she practices *retail* therapy"), but this book treats the concept of feel-good shopping with the reverence it deserves. My guess is that you probably know the many pleasures of shopping, but might be unaware of the extent to which visiting your favorite department store, online catalog, or outlet center can improve your self-image and quality of life. It's all about pinpointing what your problem is (are you jealous? unhappy with your appearance? in need of a splurge?) and learning when, how, and where to shop to maximize the psychological benefits.

First, determine what kind of shopper you are, and how therapeutic your current techniques are, by taking the *Retail Therapy Quiz* that follows. Your quiz results will guide you in choosing an appropriate retail therapy program from the many shopping solutions presented in this book.

Chapter 1: Nothing but Troubles outlines the basic concepts of retail therapy and identifies quick fixes for general states of melancholy. In other chapters, you'll encounter a range of techniques, like planning a shopping-themed vacation when you need to escape the confines of your existence or overcoming nasty feelings of jealousy at a friend's bridal shower.

And, lest you find the entire premise of this book to be unconscionably materialistic and narcissistic, you're covered in *Chapter 9: Spread the Love*, which points to the psychological benefits of giving money or donating unwanted goods to charity, shopping for people other than yourself, and other altruistic gestures.

Finally, each chapter includes a real-life *Shopper's Success Story*—proof that retail therapy works, and can work for you. Hopefully you will be inspired to follow these examples. And once you've read through this guide, my hope is that you will return to it for the perfect shopping solution whenever your mood needs perking up. There's no reason to sit and stew when a little shopping can have you whistling a happy tune in a matter of minutes.

As for me, all this writing about shopping has left me yearning for the real deal. If you need me, I'll be at T.J. Maxx.

Happy shopping,
Amy Elliott
Brooklyn, New York
April, 2006

Retail Therapy Quiz

How do you unleash the healing power of shopping? First, you need to embrace the idea that shopping can make you happy. Next, evaluate your shopping habits and attitudes. Finally, reflect on your shopping m.o. and how happy or "high" it makes you feel—surely there's room for improvement!

Here's a quiz to help you determine your shopping style—tally your responses and read the results to find out how to use the suggestions in this book most effectively.

WHAT'S YOUR SHOPPING STYLE?

1) *In general, your life is*
   a. Terrific.
   b. Tolerable.
   c. Untenable.

2) *When was the last time you went shopping?*
   a. Five minutes ago—they forced me to leave because they were closing.
   b. Last weekend—I needed to find a dress for a black-tie event.
   c. Last month—a friend dragged me to Bloomingdale's.

3) *"I get depressed when…"*

   a. I acknowledge the number of beauty products I own and never use.

   b. I open my closet and face the fact that I have "no clothes."

   c. I'm depressed 24/7.

4) *"When I'm stressed at work, I…"*

   a. Take a break and pop into the nearest Banana Republic to see what's on sale.

   b. Poke around on amazon.com or eBay.com.

   c. Cry.

5) *"When I'm in a bad mood, I…"*

   a. Make a beeline for the mall.

   b. Make a beeline for the drugstore to buy candy.

   c. Huff, puff, and make those around me uncomfortable.

6) *Friends might call you _____.*

   a. Self-indulgent.

   b. Sensible.

   c. A party pooper.

7) *"I get 'high'…"*

   a. When I buy a new pair of shoes.

   b. After an intense workout.

   c. Not applicable.

8) Which statement most accurately describes your closet?

   a. Fully stocked with quality merchandise—in fact, some of the items still have the tags on them.

   b. Misguided—I don't have much that's considered "classic."

   c. Lame—mostly hand-me-downs from my shopaholic friends and a few "good" pieces that I wear nonstop.

9) Over the years, the number of "Born to Shop" items you have received as gifts is _____ .

   a. Let's see, there's the throw pillow, the bumper sticker, the T-shirts, the stationery...

   b. Zero—but birthday cards always reference my passion for shoes.

   c. Ew, that's gross.

10) If you walked into the nearest BCBG or Bebe boutique, the sales associate would say _____ .

   a. "Hi! How've you been? Come with me, you have to see this skirt. It's perfect for you!"

   b. Nothing. She senses you're "just looking."

   c. "You lost?"

11) Ugh, the curtains in your bedroom are looking kind of ragged. You need new ones, so you...

   a. To compare prices and selection, you'll shop online, hit a department store, and pop into Anthropologie.

   b. Call your mother.

   c. Decide you don't deserve them.

12) Say your boyfriend dumps you. The next day, your friends would find you...
   a. In the dressing room at Barney's.
   b. On the StairMaster, flipping through a J. Crew catalog.
   c. In bed, sleeping off a Xanax.

13) At Saks Fifth Avenue, you spot a gorgeous Marc Jacobs jacket that's about $100 more than you want to spend. You...
   a. Buy it anyway—it will be an "investment" piece.
   b. Skip it, but spend the equivalent on a handbag, sunglasses, and a silk scarf.
   c. Eye it wistfully, then leave.

14) When was the last time you purchased a new skin-care product?
   a. Yesterday—I was feeling ugly.
   b. Last month—I needed something oil-free for summer.
   c. Two years ago—if I mix a little water into my tub of Noxema, bet I can make it last another week.

15) "When someone asks me what I paid for something, I knock off 20 to 30 dollars to save face." This statement is true:
   a. Always.
   b. Sometimes.
   c. Not applicable—it would take a lot for me to spend $20 to $30 in the first place.

If you answered...

MOSTLY A'S

You're a passionate shopper and fully aware of its therapeutic effects. Read this book to improve on and fine-tune your techniques. You've already got a solid foundation but will no doubt benefit from our streamlined, targeted approach. You know that shopping can set you up with a nice buzz, but you may not realize that there are specific kinds of retail therapy you can use in response to specific forms of emotional turmoil. Feeling fat and ugly? Flip to *Chapter 2: Don't Look Now!* for tips on buying hats, a list of guilt-free purchases, and to find out whether a manicure or a pedicure is better equipped to give your self-esteem a boost. Just broke up with someone? *Chapter 3: Heart Attack* has customized strategies galore. And if you're looking for the ultimate shopping high, *Chapter 6: Cheap Thrills* will show you how to reach shopping nirvana through skillful bargain shopping.

MOSTLY B'S

You're a committed shopper, but you're ignorant of its mood-altering potential. At this point, your shopping habits are more need-based and practical. This book will teach you a host of different ways to let your emotions dictate when you shop, where you shop, and what you buy. *Chapter One: Nothing but Troubles* reinforces the idea that shopping is a happy-making activity that you should indulge in at all times, especially when the going gets tough. The tips in *Chapter 7: You're in the Money* are predicated on the idea that saving money—and resisting temptation—is a buzz kill; you stand to experience more intense feelings of satisfaction when you drop cash on fabulous investments like fine jewelry, fine art, or a couture gown. By the time you finish reading this book, you'll have learned how to chase highs like a libertine, a true bon vivant—your troubles, as well as your somewhat abstemious mindset, may become a thing of the past forever.

MOSTLY C'S

Yikes. You have an unhealthy attitude toward shopping. Fortunately, this book will introduce you to the idea that shopping is a constructive way to spend your time because it stirs up feelings of comfort and joy, and gets your adrenaline pumping. When you're feeling low, the best thing you can do is head out to the mall or the drugstore, or log on to the internet—I promise that doing so will lift your spirits whenever depression rears its ugly head.

Employing the retail therapy techniques in this book will show you the many ways that shopping can buoy you up into a state of elation. *Chapter One: Nothing but Troubles*, which offers retail therapy strategies for when you're just generally down or in a bad mood, is a great catch-all to begin with. Once you have success with those techniques, you can move on to other chapters, where you'll be able to tackle specific woes—like a job you hate, a birthday you're dreading, or feelings of jealousy toward your well-dressed coworkers. Pay special attention to the *Success Stories* in each chapter—testimonials from real women whose inspiring retail therapy tales of triumph are sure to convince you that shopping is the key to satisfaction with yourself—and your quality of life.

CHAPTER 1

Nothing but Troubles

SHOPPING TO OBLITERATE BAD DAYS AND BLUE MOODS

When you're feeling stressed, cranky, or depressed, it's sometimes hard to put your finger on precisely what it is that's bothering you. A psychotherapist can help you identify the source, but in the meantime, why not go shopping? A trip to the mall, even to the drugstore, has the power to brighten your mood, in part because the act of shopping releases dopamine, the brain chemical associated with feelings of pleasure and satisfaction. So grab your purse and let the healing begin.

Shop at a Department Store

Although the big department stores are no longer the grand shopping palaces enjoyed by our parents and grandparents, they continue to provide marvelous opportunities to block out the moody blues. For starters, the sight of so much neatly displayed merchandise, and the knowledge that even more goods await your perusal on other floors, can inspire even the most down-in-the-dumps shopper to leave no sweater unturned. Meanwhile, ever-so-slight traces of that old-school luxury still manage to pervade the frenetic environment and bewildering infrastructure of today's department stores; the gleaming glass cases, the smell of perfume, and the cushy ladies' lounges can have an intoxicating effect on any shopper in need of a serious pick-me-up.

Besides, department stores provide all sorts of entertainment above and beyond shopping. The architecture itself might be worthy of your attention (think Printemps in Paris or Carson Pirie Scott in Chicago). Sometimes there is live piano music or a guest chef performing a demonstration in the cookware department to distract you. People-watching is pretty good fun, too. Observe how many of your fellow shoppers are taken in by semi-deceptive promotional schemes, like a sign that says "Sale:

$19.99"—with "and Up" in tiny letters underneath. And, of course, window displays have been thrilling the public for decades—especially during the holidays, when department store windows become carefully art-directed wonderlands.

Some people advocate working out when you're in a funk, and they have a point—the more strenuously you exercise, the more blissed-out you'll feel afterward. Likewise, I would argue that the longer you stay in a department store, the more likely you are to find and purchase things that'll make you smile.

Department stores are also excellent venues for tiring yourself out ("We shopped till we dropped!"), a therapeutic strategy that's sure to divert your mind from whatever's ailing you. After doing yourself in at Macy's or Marshall Field's, it's lovely to come home, drop your bags at the door, and collapse on the couch for a nap.

More reasons to seek solace in a department store:

- *You stand a good chance of finding something on sale,* which always has a rousing effect on the psyche. (See Chapter 6: Cheap Thrills for additional methods you can use to access these euphoric feelings on a regular basis.)

- *The ladies who work the makeup counters will fawn over you* and praise flatteringly specific aspects of your appearance: "Everyone should have your cheekbones," or, "I swear, you could be Scarlett Johansson's twin."

- *You can scope out guys in the men's department* with the knowledge that they have at least some concern about their appearance. (Hey, they're shopping, right?)

Retail Reels

Snowed-in? Maxed out your credit card? Rent one of these flicks—all have at least one great shopping scene that'll more than distract you from your troubles.

The Best of Everything (1959)

Breakfast at Tiffany's (1961)

Lord Love a Duck (1966)

Falling in Love (1984)

9½ Weeks (1986)

Moonstruck (1987)

When Harry Met Sally (1989)

Pretty Woman (1990)

Scenes from a Mall (1991)

Indecent Proposal (1993)

Four Weddings and a Funeral (1994)

Clueless (1995)

Vénus Beauté Institut (1999)

Serendipity (2001)

Le Divorce (2003)

Splurge on Personalized Stationery

Feeling like a nobody? Invisible or undervalued? You won't if you have a desk drawer full of luxe, personalized stationery. Instead, you'll feel important, like an ambassador to a foreign country, or pampered and entitled, as though you've spent your entire life lunching with Muffy, Bitsy, and Blake. In an era when e-mail and text messages have become the default modes of communication, custom-designed stationery will set you apart from the pack. This wasn't always the case.

At one time, every classy, well-mannered woman owned a set of monogrammed correspondence cards, or letterhead printed with her name and address in curlicued script. Personalized stationery was considered a social necessity; it conveyed that you were a person of impeccable manners, character, and taste. Thanks to the desktop publishing revolution, which made printing more affordable, you can enjoy the pleasures of chic monogrammed note cards, too.

Today there are innumerable font and paper styles to choose from, as well as a spectrum of fashionable colors and sophisticated design templates—not all of them über preppy. The proprietor of your local paperie can help you find stationery to suit your needs and personality. Cute custom-designed calling cards have become "smart" again, so be sure to include some in your order.

Hit a Drugstore

A fistful of ponytail holders. A heart-shaped box of chocolates. A red plastic basket brimming with rainbow-colored school supplies. What do these items have in common? All are bizarrely happy-making, and all are available at your neighborhood drugstore—a place that never fails to stimulate and excite the senses in powerful ways.

"I frequently recommend drugstore-shopping to my clients because it offers a pleasant diversion from everyday woes," says Jeri Kadison, a stress management and communication coach. "Plus, going to the drugstore gets you moving and out of the house, which is often the first step to eliminating doldrums." Stocking up on your favorite health and beauty supplies is always a kick. Other goodies to consider:

- **Greeting cards:** *They're colorful, corny, and so darn cute!*

- **Tabloid magazines:** *Always juicy; replenished weekly.*

- **Pretty paper goods:** *Not just for picnics.*

- **Crayons and Magic Markers:** *Reminders of carefree times.*

"It worked for me!"

ONE SHOPPER'S SUCCESS STORY

Everyone knows that drugstores can provide a chemical boost, whether it's in the form of prescription meds or Red Bull. These stores, which are open 24 hours a day in L.A., also give me a shopping high. The hair notions aisle can amuse me for hours.

Recently a good friend decided to trade in the sunny silliness of L.A. for a more stable, but much colder, life in Chicago. On our way to her going-away dinner, my friend Anne and I found ourselves despairing over the thought of our group of girlfriends splitting up. We had a little time to kill so we popped into our favorite Rite Aid for some treats to lift our spirits. Between the Sour Skittles and discounted Easter Peeps (stale but still delicious!), we soon had a sugar high that lifted us right out of the doldrums. Even better, we stumbled upon a package of five neon-rubber friendship bracelets, embossed with phrases like "friends forever." True, they were targeted at nine-year-olds, but the bracelets were a hit at dinner with all our friends. Which proves you're never too old for friendship. Or jewelry. Even neon-rubber jewelry.

—Jessica, 30, West Hollywood, California

Treat Yourself to Elegant Edibles

Most days you may be a supermarket girl like the rest of us, but one of the best places to shop when you're having a bad day is a fancy food emporium. As you survey the gourmet brands, the beautiful packaging, the exotic spices, you'll envision the brunches and dinner parties you might throw in the future—an indoor picnic for two shared in front of the fire, or an indulgent supper for one consisting of French bread, Camembert, and fine wine. Plus, it's fun to feel like a "regular," a character in a Woody Allen film, perhaps, for whom stocking up on scones, leeks, crème fraîche, a pound of pink peppercorns, and a bottle of Prosecco is standard procedure. Doesn't *everyone* buy a bouquet of farm-fresh flowers every day?

When it comes to lifting the spirits, a healthy dose of sugar is always helpful. Shopping at an upscale *confiserie* is a highly effective form of retail therapy because it allows you to indulge your craving for sweets in a luxurious setting. Immerse yourself in this intoxicating, usually French-themed environment; the

sight of so many shiny boxes adorned with satin ribbon and silk flowers will make whatever you end up purchasing feel like the most decadent splurge. There's something quite elegant about seeing exotic sweets like rose-infused marshmallows or passion fruit-flavored *pâte de fruits* delicately arranged in a pretty box—and knowing that the only person who gets to eat them is you. Of course, the handmade chocolates and marzipan molded into glossy fruit-shapes are sure to make your mouth water and your heart flutter, too.

• SOLUTION 5 •

Shop for Bedtime

When you're really out of sorts, you may feel like you want to crawl into bed and never leave. Nothing wrong with that. But if you're committed to using retail therapy strategically, you should resist the urge, at least temporarily, and start shopping. What should you shop for? Luxurious sleepwear—not the sexy stuff, but gowns and pajamas that are elegant, feminine, and comforting (I like Eileen West and Hanro of Switzerland). Picture the kind of garments a 1960s-era mother might have packed in her daughter's suitcase before shipping her off to a posh mental hospital in the country.

When you're in the midst of a meltdown that makes you want to stay in bed, purchasing a sex toy also makes sense. And fortunately, you can do this kind of shopping from the comfort of your home via the internet or catalogs. There are tons of battery-operated or plug-in goodies to choose from that are designed to stimulate you in every possible fashion (babeland.com is a great place to do your "research"). More incentives: If you have the gadget sent via FedEx, you'll soon have something to occupy yourself besides sitcom reruns, and if you've ever had trouble in the orgasm department, you'll quickly kiss those days goodbye. Best of all, when you're ready to return to the world of the living, you and your partner can play with your new "friend" together.

Embrace the Impulse Purchase

People say it's unwise to buy on impulse, but sometimes the reverse is true.* If you're fixated on a distressing situation or predicament, succumbing to an impulse purchase allows you to re-focus your anxiety; instead of your real troubles, you'll obsess over the money you just spent, or on whether or not you were right to go with the size 6 instead of the size 8, or if the Louis Vuitton bag you just bought at a flea market is a cheapo knock-off, not "vintage" at all.

A few years ago, my friend B. was a penny-saving 25-year-old on a tight budget because she'd recently been laid off by a downsizing dot-com. A mutual friend of ours got us tickets to a charity event her company had organized—high-end designers in the home furnishings industry had donated goods for atten-dees to bid on via silent auction. It was fun to ogle the offerings, but none of us was in a financial position to actually place a bid. That is, until B. fell in love with a gorgeous chair. It had a chrome frame with tufted white leather cushions, and was so sleek it might as well have been plucked from the set of a Gucci ad.

The starting bid was $500—could she afford it? Not really. After all, without a job, she had no disposable income. But this piece was perfect for her, and totally in keeping with her fondness for David Hockney prints and careworn Marimekko sheets. So we encouraged her to take the plunge. And she won (final price: $750). She was giddy and wide-eyed as she handed over her credit card—this was more money than she'd ever spent on a single item. Later she did have a minor freak-out about her purchase and how much it cost. But we were thrilled that she was no longer lamenting the loss of her job, nor was she in panic mode about the larger, more troubling issue of her next career move. When she was ready to deal, she had a great-looking chair on which to sit and stylishly contemplate her options.

Note: *This retail therapy technique should be used sparingly, and not unless directed by at least one, and preferably two, people you trust (the salesperson counts).*

CHAPTER 2

Don't Look Now!

SHOPPING TO BOOST YOUR SELF-ESTEEM

Feeling fat and ugly? Join the club. Every woman feels this way from time to time, but a negative self-image should never deter you from shopping. No, this is the time to shop for things that will a) improve your appearance, b) draw attention to the aspects of your appearance that you do like, or c) simply make you feel prettier and sexier. One important rule, though: Stay away from the dressing room—at least until you're ready to accept your imperfections.

· SOLUTION 1 ·

Splurge on Shoes

I saw a pillow in a store window recently. It said, "A new pair of shoes cures the blues." My mother is a shoe girl—and while she doesn't own that pillow, she does have one that says, "If the shoe fits, buy it in every color" displayed front-and-center in the living room. She also has a collection of miniature shoes that she displays on a knickknack shelf. And, oh yes, two closets full of size 5 shoes in every hue, shape, and style imaginable. She says her compulsion stems from a belief that a time will come when size 5 shoes are no longer in production, and worse, not even available in stores—so whenever she finds them on sale, she can't resist snatching them up. "You can't just leave them there," she says, and I know lots of other women can relate to her thought process.

Shoes are rarely about necessity, are they? Most of the time, they're about beauty and the joy that accompanies wearing and owning something beautiful. I think we buy shoes the way we would have bought Madame Alexander dolls if we'd had credit cards at age six. Shoes are also a unique elixir because they don't discriminate—you needn't be beautiful, or have a beautiful body to wear them. And yet, when you try them on and they look stunning as you strut up to the mirror, something magical happens. It's kismet. It's Cinderella sliding her foot into a slipper made of glass.

"It worked for me!"

ONE SHOPPER'S SUCCESS STORY

On an exceedingly wet and dreary day in autumn, I decided it was high time to deal with the thick bundle of utility bills I'd stashed in my purse. The weather, and a particularly unfortunate date the night before, had put me in a terrible, self-loathing mood, so I figured commencing the monthly assault on my checkbook couldn't make things much worse. Hold up—what was this black-and-white striped postcard peeking out of the stack? A forgotten announcement for…the Delman spring shoe sample sale beginning that very day! Bills be damned—I threw them on my desk, grabbed my umbrella, and took an early lunch to hit the sale, just blocks from my office.

Once I entered the first of three rooms filled with row upon row of neatly stacked glossy, black-and-white checked shoe boxes, I knew my mood—if not my checking account—would be saved that day. I surveyed this shoe-lover's dreamscape with mounting excitement, taking in the floral-printed and pastel-hued ballet flats, soft metallic strappy sandals, and open-toed suede wedge heels in eye-popping jewel tones—all at half to a third off the original prices. Best of all, there were no salespeople to pester you about sizes; you just looked for yours from the stack, hoping there was at least one pair left, and grabbed the box, which I did—over and over again.

With barely restrained glee, I jockeyed for a spot in the mirror to moon over lilac satin ballet flats, delicate black leather kitten-heel sandals, and—hottest of all—scarlet and fuchsia suede wedges with ankle straps. They all looked fabulous—so fresh and spring-y! I couldn't imagine parting with any of them, but I definitely couldn't part with what amounted to half my paycheck in one afternoon (at least not today). I wistfully discarded the glamorous, yet impractical, suede wedges, but floated my luminous flats and sandals to the register. I knew the bills would still be there when I got back, but I didn't care—I had beautiful new shoes, and all was right with the world.

—Amy V., 34, Brooklyn, New York

• SOLUTION 2 •

Buy Yourself a Hat

Hats can be attention-getting, a great thing if your self-esteem issues are linked to feelings of invisibility. At the same time, a hat can be a wonderful disguise, a sort of socially acceptable and super stylish mask to wear when a) you're having a bad-hair day; b) you have a blemish that needs concealing; or c) you want to shut out the world by seeming unapproachable and/or intimidating. Here are some basic hat-buying tips:

● *Those with round and square face shapes* should choose hats with an asymmetrical brim.

● *If you are on the plump side and also short,* choose a hat with a wide brim that you can roll up from the sides or the back to add height.

● *To downplay a large nose,* choose hats with crowns that are high in the front, which draws the eye upward, away from the nose.

● *If you have sharp, angular features,* choose hats with soft, flirty embellishments, which will tone down the hard lines.

- **When selecting a straw hat,** make sure it has dress-up potential; look for something you can wear on the beach but also to a summer wedding.

- **And here's a gem to keep in mind** from the 1938 tome Better Than Beauty: A Guide to Charm *by Helen Valentine and Alice Thompson:* "Even if the hat is not the most flattering in the world, it may well give you an air of sophisticated chic that can be better than mere prettiness."

· SOLUTION 3 ·

Focus on Accessories

"If you're feeling fat, why not shop for accessories?"

—LULU GUINNESS

Accessories are magical, and it pays to remember this when your self-esteem is plummeting. It's hard to ignore your flaws when trying on clothes, but accessories are always a love fest— which is why shopping for them is one of the most successful retail therapy techniques out there.

I'm obsessed with big rings, huge ones that I have to wear on my middle finger—one of my favorites is silver with a giant lemon topaz; another is a semi-circular dome of sky-blue rhinestones. I always wear these rings when I need to feel more confident and desirable, especially on first dates. I'm sure you own a couple of similarly "magnetic" accessories, but when your self-image needs fixing up, more is more!

● **Sunglasses** *are just...glamorous. You can never have too many pairs. And a designer pair can effortlessly transform a lackluster outfit into a luminous one. Maybe you can't afford a Marc Jacobs handbag, but a pair of his sunglasses is the next best thing.*

> *"One well-made top-quality handbag will outlive three or four cheap ones, and is therefore often a profitable investment in the end."*
>
> —Genevieve Antoine Dariaux

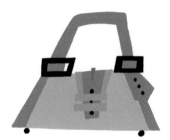

- **Handbags** are always a kick—and well worth a splurge.

- **Belts** are a wardrobe essential that are rarely on the shopping list, but almost always in short supply, even in the closet of the most well-dressed woman you know. Picking up a smart belt or two is the shopping equivalent of doing a good deed. Your mood and your wardrobe both stand to benefit from such a purchase.

- **Scarves** are always a pleasure—they're tactile, colorful, and extremely versatile. You can wear them around your neck, as a headband, as a belt or sash, even around the crown of a straw hat. I use them as curtain tie-backs and sometimes drape one over a lampshade to make the lighting more romantic.

Buy Flowers

Is there anything more pathetic than a woman buying herself flowers? Yes, so get over it. Fresh flowers are one of the cheapest thrills around, the ultimate pick-me-up when your self-esteem is suffering. Opt for blooms in shades of red and yellow, which are the most positive, energizing, and uplifting colors in the spectrum. Plus, displaying flowers in your home instantly perks up the environment and, by extension, your mood.

If that's not enough to entice you, the process of arranging the flowers in a vase might: It's a dreamy, creative process that doesn't require perfection. "I often think of flowers as a way to instantly redecorate your home without having to invest in new upholstery, paint, or wallpapering," says floral designer David Stark, coauthor of *Wild Flowers* and *To Have & to Hold*. "I like to have multiple bud vases around my house that can showcase one or two stems of varying types and sizes and colors, and group them in little vignettes, on various pieces of furniture. I just give a fresh cut, drop a beautifully arching bloom into the perfect bud vase for it, and let the flower dance toward the light." Sounds easy, right? Give it a try!

Snack Time

Pangs of hunger and dehydration can impede the retail therapy process, so make sure your purse is well stocked with sustenance. A box of cookies, a chocolate bar, or a bag of gummy candies may seem like the ideal way to increase your stamina, but if you're already having body-image issues, don't go there. Instead, try these guilt-free goodies:

- **Energy Bars** (ample supplies of protein; taste like candy!)

- **Baked potato chips**

- **Baby carrots**

- **Apple/Pear/Orange** (but bring a napkin, or, better yet, cut your fruit into slices and transport in a plastic baggie or container)

- **Turkey jerky**

- **Granola bars and cereal bars** (decadent tasting, packable, and relatively low-cal)

- **Raisins**

- **Diet Coke**

- **Water, water, water!**

Nail Call

Q. *What delivers a better high—a manicure or a pedicure?*

A. A pedicure delivers the best buzz, but they're twice as expensive as manicures and are typically sought out by women who are already pretty confident. "For them, a pedi is like icing on the cake—just a nice thing to have," says Pauline Mai, owner of the San Francisco–based Polished Lounge nail salon. "But for a girl who's feeling low, getting a manicure will lift her spirits in a quick, budget-friendly way."

So true! If you happen to be wearing closed-toe shoes, no one will see your pedicure—no matter how fabulous it may be. A manicure gets much more air-time. Most importantly, with a manicure, you will appreciate how clean and tidy your nails look and how soft your hands feel. Just looking at them will instantly make you feel more ladylike and refined.

"In terms of color, I prefer neutral shades of polish, like barely-there pinks and beiges," says Mai. "The point is to look well groomed—not overdone." For a little more zing, though, opt for cherry-red nail polish, which will revive your self-confidence and invite your inner sex-kitten to come out and play. *Rarrrw!*

Buy Lipstick

A new tube of lipstick, the more glamorous the packaging the better, will always make you feel prettier—*always*. It's a quick, inexpensive fix that improves your overall physical appearance, and consequently, your self-esteem. "Bright red shades are the way to go when you're feeling blue," says Marcia Firesten, a buyer for Palmetto, a beauty and gift boutique with locations in Los Angeles and Santa Barbara. Imagine the fun you'll have trying to find the shade that suits you best—and when you do, you'll automatically feel more sexy and confident. The screen goddesses of the forties and fifties wore brilliant-red lipstick—they were proud to flaunt their sexuality. Wear a color that pops and see what happens!

Not sure you can pull it off? "Glossy lips are the perfect fix for the blahs," says Amanda Nelson, co-owner of the Chicago-based beauty emporium Powder Room. Which formulas have the most Prozac-like effect? Pinkish hues with a glossy finish and a hint of sparkle. The color will make you look girl-next-door sweet, but the shine radiates confidence and sex appeal.

Invest in Skin Care

Your skin is your most precious attribute—you can have a killer body, great hair, a gorgeous wardrobe, and a charming personality, but skin that looks old, tired, dehydrated, or pockmarked can nullify all of your assets put together. So whenever you feel fed up with your appearance, the smartest thing you can do is upgrade your skincare regimen. For example, if you tend to use drugstore brands, make a trip to the mall and try out products from a prestige brand. If you're already a skin-care junkie and regularly shop the best makeup counters, delve deeper into your options—surely there's a new serum, eye cream, or high-tech anti-aging potion you haven't discovered yet.

If you've seen and tried it all, it might be time to make an appointment with a dermatologist—and not the kind you visit if you have a rash or a wart! Seek out a dermatologist who specializes in cosmetic dermatology who will work with you to customize a skin-care regimen that suits your needs. Together, you may decide that it's time for Botox or a micro-dermabrasion treatment; both procedures are known to dramatically improve the skin's appearance.

Buy with Confidence

Overspending, like overeating, can stir up feelings of gluttony and self-hatred in a heartbeat, which defeats the whole purpose of retail therapy. Here, a list of guilt-free purchases—practical items that need frequent replenishing or enduringly classic items you'll wear forever—that you should always feel justified in buying.

- **Cashmere sweaters** *(especially if on sale)*

- **Black trousers** *that fit perfectly*

- **Black leather high heels**

- **Tall boots** *that fit perfectly*

- **A great "work" bag**

- **White T-shirts**

- **Nude tank tops** *(for wearing under sheer tops)*

- **Umbrellas**

- **Mascara** *(every new formulation warrants a test-run)*

- **Wineglasses**

- **Hand cream**

- **Cute dish towels**

- **Pillow cases**

- **Stylish gift wrap**

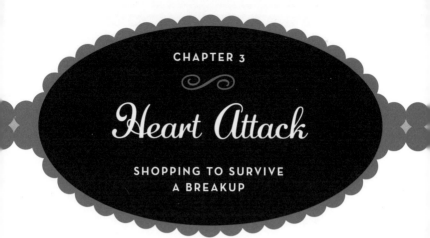

CHAPTER 3

Heart Attack

SHOPPING TO SURVIVE A BREAKUP

Put away those tissues, stop your sniveling! When you're in the midst of a painful breakup, you may think you want to sit home watching *Law & Order: Special Victims Unit* reruns with an arsenal of junk food at the ready, but you need to get out there and start shopping. Employ some or all of the retail therapy strategies that follow, and soon you'll be feeling a lot better about being on your own again—you may even forget what you saw in your ex in the first place.

• SOLUTION 1 •

Buy a New Fragrance

Shopping for perfume is nothing short of sublime. It's a uniquely elegant experience, and a great way to cure feelings of rejection, worthlessness, and despair, because the purchase itself is so utterly indulgent. Scent has the power to evoke memories, emotions, sensations, and thoughts, so when you break up with someone, replacing your old scent with a new one will also prevent you from falling prey to your olfactory associations with the failed relationship. In other words, wearing a new fragrance is a way to drape yourself in a new identity.

I recently met with New York City perfumer Alexis Karl, who told me that she originally created one of her best-selling blends, Eve's Revenge, for a friend who was going through an awful breakup. "She asked me to create a scent to lift her mood and make her feel very sensual, sexy, and sinfully delicious," says Karl. The perfume combined tart notes of pomegranate (*the* forbidden fruit!); luscious fig; dark, sexy amber; and hints of freesia. "Suffice to say, the fragrance gave my friend the sensual boost she craved," says Karl. "It elevated her mood and made her feel devastatingly sexy."

When shopping for a new scent, keep these tips in mind:

- **Never buy perfume without trying it on first;** *spray some on your wrist (or inner arm) and see how the scent "blooms" on your skin. The right perfume will work with your skin's chemistry.*

- **If you're sampling many different scents,** *sniff some coffee beans in between spritzes to clear your olfactory palate. Sniffing your sleeve will also work in a pinch.*

- **Well-known commercial perfumes** *aren't necessarily the best. Experiment with perfumes from lesser-known companies whose formulations tend to be more poetic and innovative.*

- **To enjoy your new fragrance fully,** *dab it on your wrists, the nape of your neck, the backs of your knees, and the small of your back. The scent will linger in a subtle, intriguing way.*

Buy New Lingerie

"If a woman has just broken up with someone she thought was the love of her life, she should immediately throw away all of the lingerie she wore with the schmuck she broke up with and avoid 'single syndrome'—that is, sulking around the house in an old T-shirt and sweats," says lingerie expert Rebecca Apsan, owner of La Petite Coquette in New York City. Scoring some silky new unmentionables will comfort and empower you—and reinvigorate your sex appeal. Items constructed of luxurious, sensual fabrics like chiffon, tulle, lace, and even delicate, sheer cotton are excellent choices because they'll remind you that you're a desirable, sexy woman—anyone would be lucky to be with someone as hot as you!

Thinking beyond everyday wear, this is also a great time to invest in some new erotic lingerie. Apsan suggests push-up bras with matching bottoms, anything sheer with embroidery or rhinestone embellishments, a garter belt and stockings, or a teddy with a thong back. "The key is to buy any type of sexy lingerie that'll lift both your assets and your spirits—the two work hand in hand," she says.

ATTENTION SHOPPERS

Dressing-Room Drama

Lamenting your ex has meant many pints of chocolate ice cream and, most likely, many nights of nonstop crying. As a result, you're looking a little ragged. Don't worry, it's only temporary. In the meantime, remember that the unflattering lights and mirrors in your average fitting room aren't going to do you any favors. It's best to avoid them altogether. Not going to happen? Follow these tips from Samantha von Sperling, director of Polished Social Image Consultants in New York City:

- **On the day before your shopping trip,** *apply a light self-tanner or spray tan to prevent the pasty effect caused by those horrific fluorescent fitting-room lights!*

- **Make sure you are groomed and coiffed—***taking care of this in advance of the shopping spree will allow you to focus on the task at hand, instead of obsessing about your imperfections.*

- **On the day you go shopping,** *eat a light but protein-filled breakfast. Minus the carbs, you'll look and feel less bloated.*

- **If there are mirrors** *outside of the dressing room, use those. They're more flattering and make you feel less claustrophobic.*

Spoil Your Pet

Always a source of unconditional love and loyalty, Fido or Fluffy has never been more deserving of a special treat (or a 100-percent ridiculous indulgence) than now. Your furry friend will be a lifesaver during this trying post-breakup period, and it will be impossible not to smile while shopping for some new toys or gourmet doggie or kitty edibles. I recently bought my Piglet, a peach-colored tabby with a bobbed tail that looks like a rabbit's, a life-like squirrel with a tail that squeaks. As a welcome-to-our-family gift, I bought Emma, my mother's terrier mix, some fancy pet shampoo from Penhaligon's (along with a red leather collar that she promptly ate).

Don't just hit your local pet store. Look for cute bowls, mats, and toys in the housewares departments of stores like Target and Home Goods. And why not splurge on cashmere sweaters, jeweled collars, and princess-worthy miniature beds at a super-posh pet boutique? My friend Ann and I recently stopped by a pet store on Lafayette Street and Houston in Manhattan and were delighted to see that a birthday party was going on in the next room—for a little pug! Yes, all of his friends—a golden retriever, a sheba inu, a Weimaraner, even a little tiny teacup Yorkie—had gathered for the affair, along with their humans, of course. Watching the dogs frolic was such a heartwarming sight that I plan to go back the next time one of my suitors sends me packing.

"It worked for me!"

ONE SHOPPER'S SUCCESS STORY

We shared a bed the night we broke up, a Thursday, and the next morning, he slept in while I got ready for work. I had that shaken, headachy feeling; just remembering the things we'd said to each other the night before made my eyes well up. I remember going about my usual routine—showering, coffee with the Today Show on in the background. Soon I was blow-drying my hair in front of the full-length mirror in my bedroom, and he still didn't stir. I caught a glimpse of him in the mirror and it was so hurtful to see him dozing like that, so peaceful, so unaffected. I left for work without a word and didn't speak to him for many months.

But of course I mourned the loss of him, especially on the weekends. A week after we separated, I visited a friend in Greenwich, Connecticut, and that Saturday we went shopping at the local Saks Fifth Avenue. This was when Lilly Pulitzer was at the height of her 21st-century comeback; city girls were wearing her exuberant, brightly colored miniskirts and dresses to the office. Of course the girls in Greenwich had probably been wearing

Lilly for decades, but she'd never been a part of my culture. I didn't even know that I wanted a Lilly until her printed cotton sheaths called out to me. As weird as it sounds, they seemed to understand how badly I wanted and needed to feel lighthearted and rosy-cheeked again, if only for a little while.

Everyone else in town was probably at the beach, which is why my friend and I were able to take over the fitting room. We tried on all of the dresses in our sizes, creating a rainbow pile of pink pineapples, blue orchids and butterflies, green crabs, and lime-garnished cocktails before we were through. We were giddy with thoughts of pool parties we'd never attend—two girls in a Slim Aarons photo, all bare feet and big sunglasses, raising tumblers filled with Long Island Iced Tea.

In the end, the dress I chose displayed green frogs and yellow flowers. And though it wasn't cheap, I didn't hesitate. In fact, I distinctly remember how extremely good it felt to hand over my credit card, like I was buying happiness itself.

—Deborah, 31, New York City

• SOLUTION 4 •

Shop with a Pal

A common debate among retail therapy devotees is whether you stand to get better results if you shop alone or with a friend. Most women tend to seek out, and benefit from, the company of others when they're feeling lonely and out of sorts.

I think a partner in crime is always a good thing, provided said partner has a healthy attitude about shopping. I wouldn't recommend heading out to the mall with someone who is a killjoy or a penny-pincher, or someone who has the potential to cast a disapproving, dubious eye on your self-treatment methods. A friend or sibling who shares your love of shopping, however, can enrich your shopping pleasure. The ideal shopping partner would be someone loony, lyrical, and extremely rich; someone who will inspire you, pointing you to things that will make you happy and encouraging you to buy them. Nicole Diver in F. Scott Fitzgerald's *Tender Is the Night* is the perfect embodiment of these characteristics:

Nicole bought from a great list of things that ran two pages, and bought the things in the windows besides. Everything she liked that she couldn't possibly use herself, she bought as a present for a friend. She bought colored beads, folding beach cushions, artificial flowers, honey, a guest bed, bags, scarves, love birds, miniatures for a doll's house and three yards of some new cloth the color of prawns. She bought a dozen bathing suits, a rubber alligator, a travelling chess set of gold and ivory, big linen handkerchiefs...two chamois leather jackets of kingfisher blue and burning bush from Hermes...Nicole was the product of much ingenuity and toil...She illustrated very simple principles, containing in herself her own doom, but illustrated them so accurately that there was grace in the procedure...

Of course, some women prefer to languish in solitude, and if your instinct is to mull over your situation in private and shop alone, that's certainly your prerogative.

• SOLUTION 5 •

Break the Bank

Every girl has a wish list of things she wants but can't afford. When you've suffered a breakup, there's something extremely satisfying and "I've moved on" about buying something major. So if there is a pair of earrings you've had your eye on, or some artwork in a gallery you've been mooning over, this is the perfect time to go for it. And in case no one's told you yet, whatever it is that you want to buy, yes, you DO deserve it! Why not shop for:

- *A flat-screen TV*

- *A high-tech system*

- *A new couch*

- *State-of-the-art cookware*

- *A state-of-the-art vacuum*

- *A new surfboard, snowboard, or skis*

- *Private guitar lessons*

- *A class at your local university*

- *A bottle of fine Champagne*

- *A digital camera*

- *A series of facials at your favorite spa*

- *Outrageously expensive shoes*

Shopaholic Stars

Think your love life is a disaster? Just be glad you're not one of these celebrities, all as well-known for their extravagant shopping sprees as they are for their calamitous relationships.

- *Britney Spears*
- *Paris Hilton*
- *Jennifer Lopez*
- *Michael Jackson*
- *Elton John*
- *Lindsay Lohan*
- *Nicole Richie*
- *Hilary Duff*

- *Jessica Simpson*
- *Kimora Lee Simmons*
- *Celine Dion*
- *Liza Minnelli*
- *Beyoncé Knowles*
- *Lil' Kim*
- *Star Jones Reynolds*
- *Victoria Beckham*

• SOLUTION 6 •

Buy New Bedding

Since it's the main attraction, your bed dictates the vibe of your boudoir. And now it's a repository for all these memories of you and your ex tangled in the sheets, lazing around on a Sunday morning, or snuggling on a cold winter's night. Ick. Give your bed a makeover—and quickly. Shopping for, and purchasing, new bed linens (and a dust ruffle, too, perhaps?) will infuse your bedroom with positive energy. Some pointers:

● **Make sure your sheets are 100-percent cotton,** *preferably Egyptian cotton—the best you can afford. Highly durable, lustrous, and silky, these luxe sheets are made of extra-long fiber staples grown along the Nile River.*

● **What's the deal with thread count?** *Thread count refers to the number of threads per square inch and helps determines the quality of a sheet. High thread-count sheets (300 plus) are long-lasting and exceptionally soft (lower thread-count sheets have a "scratchy" feel and take longer to break in).*

- **Don't want to ditch your fancy down comforter?** *Just buy a duvet cover (also called a comforter cover), which slips over your comforter like a pillowcase. They're about half the price of a new comforter and easy to launder, too.*

- **Installing a canopy** *or a cascade of netting above and around your bed instantly creates an ultra-romantic vibe.*

- **Buy some linen spray—***slipping into lightly scented sheets is a luxury you should experience every single night!*

Women constantly compare themselves to one another, whether it's a petty, "Honey, you are so much prettier than her!" or a wistful, "God, I wish I had your legs." Call it human nature, or a deep-rooted, survival-of-the-fittest compulsion to squash our fellow females in the game of looking good and getting attention. Yet for some reason, when it comes to scoring the very best purchases at the very best prices, things have a tendency to get out of hand. Here are some familiar people and situations that tend to trigger feelings of jealousy and insecurity—and shopping strategies to help you cope.

Coping with Show-Offs

At our core, we're competitive hunters, which is why one woman's shopping triumph often means another woman's resentment. Recently, while at a photo shoot for the magazine I work for, I found myself chatting with a couple of the models. All were about 19 years old and impossibly thin and gorgeous, but this didn't bother me. Instead, I became disgruntled when one of the models, a blonde who'd flirtatiously posed for the camera with one of her eyebrows slightly raised, her glossy, parted lips set in a defiant pout, casually mentioned that she'd been to an amazing sample sale over the weekend. "Yeah, a friend of mine works for Gucci," she said. "I mean, their sales are really exclusive but she got me in, and all of the shoes were, like, $40. I bought five pairs."

Her fellow models nodded approvingly, but my skin was crawling. I pictured this statuesque beauty trying on strappy stilettos, Grecian-looking sandals, and monogram flats, an image that might have ushered me into a pleasant daydream about what I might have found that day had I been well-connected enough to attend such a glamorous caper. But instead I was just...jealous!

How did I handle these irrational, not to mention extremely shallow, feelings? That night, I logged onto eBay, where there were plenty of Gucci shoes, even in my popular size (6½), on offer. Most cost a lot more than $40. Still, it was a comfort to know that if I really, really had to have a pair of Gucci shoes, I could get my hands on a pair quite easily. And I wouldn't have to pay full price. (Whenever you feel you've missed out on the deal of the century, eBay always serves up something similar, or better.)

Pangs of shopping envy are common, and mercifully short-lived, but when you catch yourself turning green, try to deal with these feelings as soon as possible. If a coworker shows up on a Monday with a brand-new silk blouse she bought over the week-end and you find yourself coveting it, there's no shame in finding out where she got it, and then heading out to pick up the same one in your size. Because by the time you get around to doing this, you probably won't even want the blouse anymore—in fact, something else in the store, a discovery all your own, will call out to you. And then it will be someone's turn to envy you.

"It worked for me!"

ONE SHOPPER'S SUCCESS STORY

There was this fabulous copper-colored leather satchel from Banana Republic that I'd been eyeing for a month. I first spotted it in the window of the Fifth Avenue store and knew I had to have it. It has dark brass hardware (so I could wear it with my silver and gold jewelry), and a wide, comfy shoulder strap (for me, this is a must). Also, it looked large enough to fit all of my stuff (I hate it when your bag is so full it looks like an overstuffed football).

When I finally went in and checked the price, my heart sank: $178 was way more than I could or wanted to spend. So I resisted temptation and moved on, which seemed like the right thing to do. And then, a week or so later on the way to work, I spotted a woman wearing "my" bag and it really bothered me (and the fact that it looked amazing with her navy blue cashmere coat didn't make me feel any better). What was even more annoying was that I knew I could have marched over to Banana Republic immediately after I got off the subway. Buying that bag was that easy. And yet I headed straight to the office, as usual.

The sight of that woman had put a bee in my bonnet, though, and I couldn't stop thinking about her—had she casually handed over her credit card like it was no big deal? Maybe her boyfriend had bought it for her. Maybe, like me, she'd coveted the bag for weeks but instead of walking away, she decided to go for it. These thoughts depressed me and reminded me of being at summer camp when I was 13: The cute guy everyone liked would be talking to me, but if a prettier girl approached, I would always defer to her. I'd step aside and kind of slink away while she tossed her hair and flirted like a pro.

After several days of indecision, I was having a crummy day at work and decided to see about the bag. (The fact that Banana Republic's merchandise tends to sell out quickly was also causing me major anxiety!). I took a $15 gift certificate I'd been saving with me, and when I arrived at the store and saw that the bag was still available, I found that I couldn't live without the object of my affection/obsession any longer.

Here's the best part: When the saleswoman rang it up, to my delight it was only $60 bucks! It was on sale, and with my discount, I paid only $45. As I handed over the cash, I felt triumphant, invincible—that woman on the subway had nothing on me.

—Amber, 30, New York City

Outsmarting a Secretive Sally

Everyone knows a Secretive Sally. She's the well-dressed, impec-cably accessorized friend or coworker who replies with a vague, "Oh, I don't remember," whenever you ask the innocent ques-tion: "Where did you get that?"

Another typical Secretive Sally move: She's just come back from lunch carrying a massive brown-and-white striped shop-ping bag from an exclusive shop and she scurries into her office, hoping you don't see her.

"Hey, big spender," you say, when you spot the bags stashed in the corner.

"Oh, they're having their eighty-percent-off sale," she says, feigning indifference.

"And you didn't tell me?"

"I thought you knew."

Secretive Sally is elusive, a lone hunter, and fiercely com-petitive. Most people hear about a sale or a special offer and tell everyone they know, but Secretive Sally always keeps this kind of info to herself. Why is she like this? Because letting you in on the where and when would be a conflict of interest—you might make out with something that is rightfully "hers." There's also this very subtle superiority thing at work: She actually thinks you don't deserve to know about the sale. What, you didn't you know that Secretive Sally is the only one worthy of wearing Dolce & Gabbana?

The best way to handle Secretive Sally is to ignore her—and then learn how to think and shop like her. Where is she getting her information?

- **Fashion magazines.** *Secretive Sally reads them religiously. Is H&M opening a location at your local mall? The Style section of your newspaper considers this headline news.*

- **Fashion-forward websites and blogs** *that advertise sales. She's a subscriber, you should be, too.*

- **Store mailing lists.** *Always say "yes" when a salesperson asks if you want to join their mailing list—this is how you hear about sales and special in-store events.*

- **Word of mouth.** *Secretive Sally is not above calling or e-mailing stores and showrooms directly to find out if and when any sales are scheduled. Take a cue and do your research, too.*

Shopping Etiquette

For every positive encounter with a fellow shopper (a murmur of approval, or an enthusiastic whoop while trying on clothes in a community dressing room, for example), there's a negative one lurking around the sales rack. Caught up in the thrill of hunt, some shoppers unwittingly assault those around them with rude and annoying behavior. Are you one of those shoppers? I hope not. Just for the record, here are the rules.

- *If your cell phone rings while you're talking to a sales rep, don't answer it. It's rude. And don't shop with the thing permanently glued to your ear. Do you know how annoying it is to hear you yapping?*

- *Be aware that your makeup may stain any clothes you slip on over your head, and that the buckle of your watch strap, even the prongs of your engagement ring, can snag delicate fabrics.*

- *Don't blame employees for a store's outlandish prices, out-of-stock items, or mislabeled goods—these things are beyond their control.*

- **If you've accidentally bumped** a purse off a shelf or knocked a dress off a rack, pick it up.

- **Likewise, if you've changed your mind** about a purchase, don't set it down just anywhere. Put it back where you found it.

- **Never bark at pushy sales people,** no matter how persistent they are. When saying "I'm just looking" isn't enough to put him or her off, look the salesperson in the eye and say, "I'll find you if I need you." Or try (said brusquely), "I'm all set."

- **A last-minute change of heart** about an item is perfectly acceptable, even after you've reached the cash register, as long as you're courteous and quick about your final decision. However, saying, "Oh, I forgot something; I'll be right back" is inconsiderate to everyone waiting in line. Don't do it.

- **Gift-wrap lines** can be long and unpleasant during the holiday season. If you're having more than three or four packages wrapped in a single session, be courteous to those who need to get in and out of that gift-wrap line in a hurry—do your shopping during off-peak hours.

• SOLUTION 3 •

Surviving a Bridal Shower

It's nothing to be proud of, but watching a friend or family member open up gift after beribboned gift at a bridal shower can be difficult, even if the bride is a terrific gal who deserves every single one of those gifts and more. Look, don't waste your time feeling bitter (especially when there are tea sandwiches and pastries awaiting your attention on a nearby table). But after the shower, you can go out and get yourself a set of monogrammed bath towels if it will make you feel better, or splurge on a cut-crystal fruit bowl, or even a sterling hostess set from Tiffany & Co. Otherwise, just try to keep things in perspective: Your time will come.

"Envy and jealousy don't make a person happy," says Victoria Moran, life coach and author of *Creating a Charmed Life*. "For your own sake, then, as much as for the bride-to-be, use your energy to send her every good wish you can come up with. She's bravely entering into an arrangement that has a 50 percent chance of success, and an equal chance of failure. She needs every positive thought you can send her. Besides, 'what goes around comes around' didn't get to be a cliché for nothing. If you want to get married, celebrate friends who are getting married. If you want a better job, celebrate friends who get promoted, and then wait for your turn."

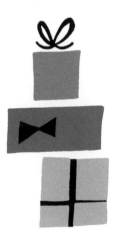

Other People's Purchases

"To this day, my sister and I are still trying to find the boots Molly Ringwald was wearing in *The Breakfast Club*!" a friend said to me recently. Perhaps you, too, can relate to this kind of merry chase. But it's one thing to covet something a celebrity is wearing and quite another to be envious of a purchase made by someone you know and love. Here, a handful of real-life encounters with the green-eyed monster that may seem familiar:

"My sister is just a couple of years older than me and there was a period of time, when I was in college and she'd graduated, during which her clothes were consistently cuter and cooler than my own. She had this cotton Laura Ashley jumper with the prettiest floral print that I was obsessed with for the longest time."

—Jennie, 35, Evanston, Illinois

"My coworker returned from a vacation in London with the most amazing rainbow-colored Missoni scarf she'd picked up on sale at Harrods. I used to tease her and say things, like, 'Oh, I see you're wearing my scarf today,' and to be honest, I was only half-joking."

—Stella, 27, Portsmouth, New Hampshire

"My friend came back from a trip to an outlet mall and she'd done especially well at the Neiman Marcus Last Call store. As she showed me her purchases, I was mostly thrilled for her—until she produced a gorgeous black-and-white checked taffeta sundress (I think it was by Nanette Lepore). A steal at $25. I can't get it out of my head!"

—Abby, 33, Englewood Cliffs, New Jersey

"I needed a raincoat, and my sister and I went to every store in the mall looking for one, but without success. On the way home, we stopped by a tag sale and, before long, my sister found an adorable, retro-looking maroon raincoat, knee-length, with a nice big belt for just $5. My sister ended up buying it for herself because I just didn't like the idea of wearing something used. And when we got home, we realized that the original tags were still on the coat. It had never been worn!"

—Elisa, 26, Cary, North Carolina

Can't Afford What You Want? Keep on Shopping

No matter how dedicated you are to shopping, feeling like the ultimate "have not" is never fun. Fashion magazines show impossibly beautiful garments with impossibly expensive price tags, celebrities score bags of swag worth thousands of dollars at awards shows, and some of your dearest friends and relatives may have paychecks double, or even triple, your own. Rather than trying to keep up financially, consider the fact that window-shopping and browsing are often just as pleasurable as the act of purchasing. Scientists have confirmed that what really gets us going is not new stuff but the anticipation of acquiring something new. So, instead of whimpering about what you can't afford, try reveling in an anticipatory state.

Also, try to think of "just looking" at luxury goods as a form of research (rather than a masochistic exercise that leaves you feeling more deprived). And in this sense, familiarity breeds contentment: Even if you can't afford to buy a Birkin handbag, you can still be an expert in the hallmarks of its construction, its history as an iconic status symbol, and on the kind of women who carry them today. In other words, you can become a connoisseur with-out spending any money. This up-market research will also come in handy when shopping at places better suited to your budget. My friend L. once spotted a pair of gold-and-diamond earrings at a Fifth Avenue jewelry store and memorized what they looked like to the letter, so that she could get the look for less some-where else (she did—but I can't say where!).

CHAPTER 5

Change Is Good

SHOPPING TO MAKE A FRESH START

You'd give your right arm to partake in an Oprah-financed makeover. You frequently consider moving to another city or country, and, in general, you'd sell your soul for the chance to go back in time and start your life over from scratch. Sound familiar? Don't get caught up in the drama of your existential crisis. What you really crave is change. For a quick fix, try giving your wardrobe an overhaul. Go shopping, try on things you wouldn't normally try on, or explore some of these other strategies to help you see yourself (and your life) in a new and improved light.

• SOLUTION 1 •

You Can't Stand Your Job

You dad may be able to give you sage advice on how to deal with a job you dislike, but for short-term relief the dedicated shopper knows that retail therapy is the only way to go. (That's what lunch breaks are for, right?) Why not focus your attention on finding a new interview outfit? Even if you don't have any interviews lined up, you'll feel practical-minded (and deliciously subversive) when you sashay by your boss with a new suit in tow. Your new threads may even motivate you to take your job search to the next level. Some tips to keep in mind:

- **Suits are always, always correct.** *Even if you're interviewing at a creative or laidback firm, wearing a suit shows that you are a true professional who respects your interviewer. You can always punch up a suit with fashionable shoes and accessories to project your style and wit.*

- **Avoid dresses.** *A tailored sheath is okay, but be sure to pair it with a coordinating blazer.*

- *Solid colors are an easy way to look "put together."* Black, navy, and gray are always safe bets. Shades of ivory, beige, and camel are also excellent choices. For a bit of color, try blue-gray, pale pink—or even a shade of red. Just be sure the color flatters your skin tone.

- *Buy a good-quality bag.* It should work well with a variety of ensembles and be large enough to hold copies of your resume, portfolio, bottled water, and other interview essentials.

• SOLUTION 2 •

You Hate Where You Live

Getting sick of your surroundings? It happens. If you're already a homeowner, call your real estate agent and get him or her on the case immediately. If you rent your place, trading up your "lame apartment" for property you actually own can be a daunting task. Ready to take the plunge? Here are some tips to help you land your new pad:

1. ***Learn real-estate lingo.*** *Attend a class (check for programs in your area) that'll give you a crash course on the sometimes-intimidating world of home buying.*

2. ***Create a wish list.*** *Include your ideal location (think of your morning commute, distance to the mall...), size (how many bedrooms and baths?), amenities (hardwood floors or carpeting?), and condition (can you deal with a fixer-upper?).*

3. ***Choose a real estate agent*** *who's used to working with first-timers. And be sure you have a good rapport with him or her.*

4. ***Be realistic.*** *If you can't afford park views and vaulted ceilings, don't waste your time—or break your own heart—by viewing homes with these features.*

5. **_Plan to save enough cash_** for a 5 to 10 percent down payment on your new home. Don't forget to factor in closing costs—usually 1 to 4 percent of the total mortgage. These may include a property appraisal, a land survey, and a pest inspection. Closing the deal may also include a prepayment of a portion of your homeowners' insurance and real estate taxes.

6. **_Consider applying for mortgage prequalification_** through your bank or a mortgage lender. You'll be one step closer to clinching the deal when you find the home you want to purchase. Just be sure to keep your credit in check—a poor report may factor negatively into the rates you are quoted.

7. **_When you're shopping for a homeowners insurance policy—_** which you'll need to have in place at the time of your closing— you may find you'll get the best rate through your current rental (or auto) insurance provider.

8. **_Once you've found your dream home,_** don't be afraid to negotiate the asking price. You can also request that needed repairs be deducted from the total cost.

SOLUTION 3

Your Car Is Ghetto

My friend Jessica recently purchased a new car, in part because something of indeterminate origin had spilled in her old one, leaving a foul odor that smelled like mildewy gym shoes and sour milk mixed with vanilla-scented air freshener. The stench lingered for months—it was there when she drove to work in the morning, and there to greet her on her way home. How could Jessica possibly derive any pleasure out of life, or accomplish her goals, when her car was suffocating her?

She realized that she needed a fresh start—and knew that a brand-new, fresh-smelling car would provide just that. Suffice it to say, her new ride not only smells fantastic, but also looks and runs better than the other one ever did. And so does Jessica! If your current car is causing you agita, here's how to score yourself a set of wheels that treats you right:

1. ***Determine what type of vehicle suits your needs**—and your budget. Visit a car-buying information site like edmunds.com; it'll give you the standard features on every new vehicle as well as information on any applicable rebates. Also browse through consumer publications to find out how well your ideal vehicle ranked in crash tests and other safety evaluations.*

2. **When you've found a car** you're interested in, it's a good idea to call your insurance agent to see how much your rate would go up if you decided to buy it.

3. **Ready for that test-drive?** Dealers' busiest times are at the end of a month, so try to schedule your visits toward the beginning of the month. Salespeople may also be more flexible then, since they love to start the month with high sales.

4. **Haggle.** Your goal is to get the largest possible discount off the sticker price, which is the manufacturer's suggested retail price (MSRP). A car that's $300 to $500 below the MSRP is considered a good deal.

5. **Never leave a dealership** with a car on your first trip. (Fortunately, shopping around is something you love to do.)

6. **Be sure that all taxes and registration fees** are included in your final quotes.

7. **If you feel like you're not getting the respect** from a salesperson that, say, a man would, don't be afraid to walk away. There's plenty of competition out there!

· SOLUTION 4 ·

You Need to Escape... Everything!

Work sucks? Check. Relationship sucks? Check. Family sucks? Check. Hair sucks? Check. Hit the gym, hit the sauce, do what you gotta do, but it sounds like what you really need is a vacation. Unfortunately, budgets mean most of us are limited in our choice of destinations. Here's how to maximize your spending power so you can enjoy the rejuvenating getaway you deserve.

1. ***Sign up for a credit card*** *that awards frequent-flyer miles based on the number of dollars you spend. You won't believe how quickly you'll be racking up those miles!*

2. ***Save time and money*** *by using travel-booking websites like Expedia, Travelocity, and Orbitz. For the best deals, be flexible with your arrival and departure dates and times.*

3. ***Submit a bid*** *on Priceline.com or SkyAuction.com. For best results, select an amount that's 20 to 30 percent off the lowest fare you find on the online booking sites.*

4. **Try to snag your lowest fare** as soon as possible—rates can change in a matter of minutes.

5. **If you like to eat, drink, and be merry,** stay at an all-inclusive resort. Your room rate, often based on a double occupancy, includes all meals and snacks, gratuities, and beverages (including booze). Imagine going to dinner without having to bring your wallet or worry about ordering that extra piña colada. Paradise, indeed.

"Get me out of here!"

Like many passionate shoppers, your checking account may not permit the super-luxurious vacation you deserve. Well, touring a city like New York, Miami, Rome, or Paris in grand style is possible if you take advantage of the latest travel trend—house and apartment swapping. This means that you temporarily trade spaces with someone living in or near the city you want to visit—and vice versa. Most trades occur in the United States, Europe, and Canada—but with a little digging, you can also find places to stay in South America, Australia, and Asia.

So how do you advertise your pad? There are a number of websites (like homeinvite.com and homelink.org) that specialize in home exchanges. Craigslist.org offers a free service (click on the "Housing Swap" link), but its listings can be hit or miss. Sure, it requires a leap of faith to hand over your house keys to a virtual stranger. But it's likely your fellow swapper has the same reservations. To get a sense of your exchange mate's personality (and potentially sketchy m.o.), spend some time chatting on the phone and correspond via e-mail. If he or she checks out, just think: All the money you'll save on lodging can be put toward fine dining, sightseeing, and, of course—lots of shopping!

• SOLUTION 5 •

You're Getting Old(er)

Those milestone birthdays are bittersweet, aren't they? On the one hand, they're cause for celebration, a chance to toast the person you've become and the life you've led thus far. At the same time, though, they mark the passage of time, inspiring wistful thoughts of missed opportunities and possibly anxiety about your mortality. Forget champagne—a little "happy birthday to me" retail therapy will get you in the mood to party in no time! I spent some time brainstorming with image consultant, stylist, and personal shopper Michelle T. Sterling of Global Image Group in New York City and San Francisco about the ideal presents to buy yourself at age 25, 30, 40, and 50.

AGE 25

A woman turning 25 should be thinking about practicality, not indulgences. Choose one or several of the five "basic blacks:"

- *A classic black suit—right for any situation, from an interview to after-work cocktails*

- *A "little black dress"*

- *A nice pair of classic black pumps*

- *A simple black leather tote*

- *A classic watch with a black leather strap*

AGE 30

Now that you've been working for a few years, you probably can afford to add more variety to your look. Consider:

- *Anything with a splash of color—liven up your wardrobe with hints of red, pink, light blue—or even coral*

- *A sexy pair of designer sling-backs*

- *At least one classic designer handbag*

- *A high-end watch—think Omega, Rolex, even Cartier*

- *Diamond studs or a classic pearl necklace*

AGE 40

Choose clothes and accessories that fit your lifestyle. You want to look youthful yet age-appropriate. Facials and other complexion-enhancing spa treatments are a great birthday treat. Otherwise, splurge on:

- **High-quality, stylish clothing—**you've graduated from the chains: go designer!

- **A diamond watch**

- **A sexy dress—**hey, if you've still got a killer body at 40, don't be afraid to show it off!

- **Bold jewelry** with semi-precious stones

AGE 50

By this age, you should be working less and living it up more. Your wardrobe should focus on comfort with a bit of glamour thrown in. Treat yourself to:

- **A couture garment—**the ultimate investment piece

- **A diamond necklace** and matching bracelet

- **Designer accessories** that complement your personality—whether that's Christian Louboutin shoes or a Chanel handbag

You Hate Your Clothes

I don't typically say, "I hate my clothes." All too often, what I do find myself saying is, "I have no clothes." This is because my closet is full of one-offs: a lilac tulle party dress, skirts that are too short for the office, flirty tops that don't work for first dates because I'll look like I'm trying too hard. It's very difficult to work these pieces into normal outfits.

If you suffer from this problem, too, have your most fashionable friend come over and put together a series of outfits for you. Thanks to her fresh, discerning eye, the contents of your wardrobe will soon start shimmering in a different light. Together, you can note the "missing" items that might work with the neglected items (say, a dark green velvet skirt to wear with a rarely-worn green and white striped chiffon blouse) and then shop stores that stand the best chance to deliver. Meanwhile, you can remove the less popular items with little to no potential (organizing experts, God bless them, say if you haven't worn it in a year, get rid of it) and donate them to Goodwill or the Salvation Army. See *Chapter 9: Spread the Love* for more charitable tips.

Yet another option, and one that I love, is to organize a clothing swap. Invite four or five girlfriends who are confronting similar closet issues (it's best if they're about the same size as you and have great taste) to your home and ask them to bring a couple of bags' worth of clothing and accessories they no longer wear. When they arrive, organize the goods according to category (shirts and tops, shoes, handbags, et cetera), crack open a bottle of wine, and everyone can start rummaging through each other's castoffs. Then, simply donate any leftovers to charity.

"It worked for me!"

ONE SHOPPER'S SUCCESS STORY

I had been invited to a fancy Valentine's Day tea at the Ritz-Carlton Hotel in Chicago and the invitation requested that ladies wear red. I have a red dress I could have worn but was in the mood for something new, and not too expensive.

A few weeks before the event, I was in New York City on business and ducked into the H&M on Fifth Avenue. There, I looked around for anything in the pink or red category that would catch my eye. I tried to ignore what I usually gravitate toward: loose-fitting tops in shades of black or charcoal gray. Then I spotted a shirt in the most gorgeous shade of candy/lipstick pink I have ever seen. But up close I saw it was the kind of top I never wear: tight and low cut, with body-hugging ruching around the waist. (At least the three-quarter-length sleeves were modest.)

For once the dressing-room line at the H&M wasn't a mile long, so I thought, well, why not try it on? So I did, and couldn't believe how I looked. Some clothes make you smile at yourself, and this top definitely did that for me. The color was tailor-made for a dark-haired, dark-eyed, olive-skinned person like me. Sure, the fit was closer than I usually wear, but the wrap style and ruching did all the right things to all the right places. And all that for twenty bucks. It was one of those cheap-chic finds that looks a lot more expensive than it is.

I wore it to the tea party with a slim black skirt and pointy boots, and got lots of compliments from lots of women. And as we know, those are the only kind that matter.

—Lisa Bertagnoli, author of *Scarlett Rules: When Life Gives You Green Velvet Curtains, Make a Green Velvet Dress and 23 Other Life Lessons Inspired by Scarlett O'Hara*

CHAPTER 6

Cheap Thrills

SHOPPING FOR ECSTASY AT BARGAIN PRICES

Shopping to overcome depression, anxiety, and ennui is emotionally healthy, but remember: Retail therapy is really about the quest for pleasure. And when it comes to pleasure, a bargain is as good as it gets, because buying items on the cheap intensifies the effects, like watching your favorite TV show in the company of your best friends, or eating crème brûlée after making love. Fortunately, bargain goods are never in short supply—if you know where to find them. Here's the straight dope on where you're most likely to score.

Become a Regular at Off-Price Stores

If you like something I'm wearing, I probably bought it at T.J. Maxx. People can't believe it. They think the racks are full of junk, but, in fact, if you're willing to persevere and dig for a few hours, you will be handsomely rewarded with more than a few dazzling finds. Name a sought-after designer or brand, I've probably spotted it, tried it on, or purchased it at T.J. Maxx once or twice. Their jewelry counter, for example, is second to none.

Marshall's, Burlington Coat Factory, Home Goods—any store that operates under the "brand names for less" principle (often up to 60 or 70 percent off retail)—is always worth your time and energy. Look at it this way: You've got $100 to spend. Would you like to go to a department store and buy a single sweater or a pair of earrings? Or, would you rather spend it on a pair of designer shoes ($39.99), a brand-name frying pan ($15), a complete outfit for your baby nephew ($21.99), gourmet jam ($3.99), cute note cards ($5.99), and a blouse from the clearance rack ($12.99)?

At an off-price store, part of the fun is that each item's price tag shows you the original suggested retail price, which can

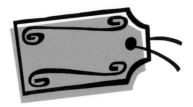

make you feel like a savvy shopper and justify any and all purchases you wish to make on that particular store visit (even if you're being more extravagant than usual). As a rule, suburban locations tend to be less picked over. If you have access to numerous suburban locations, those situated in remote, off-the-radar towns will have a better selection.

When visiting these stores, shop with an eye for well-known labels—doing so makes it easier to scan the racks. And as a rule, you really can't go into these stores looking for anything specific—you won't find sandals to wear with the dress you're wearing to your cousin's wedding, but may find last season's leather jacket for less than $50. The only strategic step you can take is to subscribe to your favorite discount chain's online mailing list, which will notify you of clearance markdowns and "new arrivals" via e-mail. Then again, the mystery, the never knowing what you're going to find, is part of the thrill.

Hold Out for End-of-Season Sales

Here's a case where timing is everything. Scoring discounted merchandise at your favorite stores may seem like a lost cause, but not if you hold out for those wonderful end-of-season sales. Here's how it works: Spring and summer merchandise usually goes on sale in June and July, and fall and winter items usually get marked down in January. Also remember that when demand is high, prices are high—and vice versa. With this in mind, you can expect bargains on these items during the following months:

- *Winter apparel, accessories, and boots:* Late December and early January

- *Summer apparel, swimsuits, and sandals:* August and September

- *Cocktail dresses:* late December and January

- *Jewelry, perfume, and lingerie:* February (after Valentine's Day)

- **Silver, watches, and picture frames:** *May*

- **White sales (bedding, rugs, towels, et cetera):** *January*

- **Home appliances:** *December through January*

- **Electronics:** *Late December through February*

- **Furniture:** *September*

Use this information strategically: It's always good to have a little notebook handy to jot down items you're interested in and where and when you spotted them. If you return to check out these items periodically, you may be able to snag them for the sale price. My cousin's friend Nicole kept "visiting" a pair of pants at Banana Republic, until one day, she came in and found them on the clearance rack for next to nothing. This was years ago, but her eyes still light up as she remembers the joy of victory.

• SOLUTION 3 •

Find an Outlet (Center)

Typically located in far-flung suburban towns near a major interstate highway, these discount shopping meccas have a heady, amusement-park quality that will make you feel like the proverbial kid in a candy store. Only the "candy" is yummy designer merchandise of the highest order (Miu Miu, Bottega Veneta, Chanel, La Perla...). Among these heavy hitters, you can also score goods from Ann Taylor, Jones New York, Nike, The Gap, J. Crew, and other everyday favorites. Here is some advice that will stand you in good stead on your next trip to an outlet center:

● **Few of us have the time to outlet-shop every week,** *so these trips require careful planning and are often an all-day commitment. Making a list of the stores you want to check out in advance will prevent you from getting sidetracked. (There's nothing worse than blowing your entire wad at BCBG, only to find that there was a Betsey Johnson lurking around the corner, and a Theory on the other side of the complex.)*

● **Visit the stores that tend to be the most energy-draining first.** *(Off Fifth and Neiman Marcus Last Call will be impossible to navigate if you're the least bit tired.)*

- **Shop with an eye for basics,** classics, and pieces that can be worn year-round.

- **Make sure you're on your favorite stores' mailing lists—**and expect postcards advertising exclusive previews, new shipments, and discount coupons galore.

- **Don't be put off by an item labeled "irregular"**—this just means that there is a minor imperfection in the garment in question. So minor, in fact, that it's probably imperceptible.

- **As a rule, sale racks** are located at the back of the store.

- **Don't shop with clothing and accessories exclusively on the brain,** even though these are the most fun to buy. Le Creuset, Waterford, Lenox, Frette, and Pratesi are just a few of the most desirable houseware brands with outlet locations.

- **If you're shopping with a group,** be sure to synchronize watches and make sure all of you have your cell phones on.

- **Last but not least:** Unless you want to spend two hours getting out of a parking lot (as I did one holiday weekend), limit your visits to weekdays.

Tripping Out

When it comes to finding bargains, distance should never be an obstacle. These destinations are among your best bets for the ultimate shopping trip:

1. ***Mall of America, Minneapolis, Minnesota:*** *This mega-mall in Minnesota has more than 500 stores, which means sales racks galore.*

2. ***Las Vegas, Nevada:*** *Forget gambling! The real draw is the Fashion Outlets of Las Vegas, where prices for high-end designer merchandise are reduced up to 75 percent off retail.*

3. ***Paris, France:*** *The city has biannual sales every winter and summer when stores significantly mark down their merchandise—up to 90 percent off retail.*

4. ***Hong Kong:*** *This energetic city is a bargain shopper's paradise. Visit in summer or winter and receive fabulous discounts from even the best stores—a VIP card from the tourist board will earn you even further discounts.*

SOLUTION 4

Seek Out a Sample Sale

Discounts are always delightful, but nothing compares to "wholesale"—the price of an item before it gets marked up by a retailer (that is, about 50 percent of what you usually pay). And the only place you can get goods for or below the wholesale price is at a designer sample sale. Here's how to shop like a pro:

- **Dress properly.** *Stripping down in front of strangers is par for the course at sample sales. Wear a skirt (but skip the thong), so you can slip on pants and skirts underneath quickly and easily without anyone catching so much as a glimpse of your booty.*

- **Sales are usually final**—*and bring cash, as sometimes credit cards aren't accepted (you can call ahead to find out for sure).*

- **Long lines**—*the length of an entire city block is not uncommon— so for best results, arrive early. And while you wait, don't let any discouraging rumors you hear about the goods or prices dissuade you. Sometimes tunnel vision can be a good thing.*

• SOLUTION 5 •

Win Big at eBay

EBay is great because the selection is so expansive. Looking for pink wedges? They've got 1,803 items that fit that description. A Diane von Furstenberg dress? Try 924. They also have great vintage clothes that mimic Marc Jacobs, Chloe, and Zac Posen looks quite effectively for a fraction of the price.

Then there's the added element of excitement that comes with placing bids and outsmarting your fellow eBayers. At the close of an auction, when the bidding can be cutthroat, I've had my cousin bid on my behalf when I couldn't be there to do so myself. You get anxious, you're checking the auction every few minutes to see if anything has changed. All of this ancillary excitement makes receiving the "You won eBay item: Lovely Eyelet & Lace Edwardian White Blouse (8396753886)" e-mail in your inbox a terrific high. Add to that the cheap prices—$11.99 for a vintage Lanvin belt, $29 for a pair of Justin cowboy boots—and…well, like me, you may just become addicted.

"It worked for me!"

ONE SHOPPER'S SUCCESS STORY

When it was my turn to buy a wedding dress, I knew there'd be no childhood friends gushing over the sight of me in a pouffy white ball gown, no chubby aunts dabbing tears from the corners of their eyes. Instead, my objective was to find a dress by a hot designer for an enviably low price.

I took off work to go to the Badgley Mischka sample sale. I arrived early and waited in line with the usual suspects—suburban women trolling for sequined dresses to wear to Bat Mitzvahs and charity balls. Inside, I was dazzled by the glittering, floor-length gowns, but it was the tags with giant red slashes that really gave me goose bumps. Before long, I emerged from the fray carrying a white dress embroidered with blue flowers. One sleeve was torn to shreds, but at $250 marked down from $5,000, this problem seemed trivial.

As I stood on another endlessly long line to pay, I imagined what my wedding might be like. I pictured round tables topped with indigo tablecloths. I could serve guests blueberry gelato between courses. Then, the loudest explosion I'd ever heard shook me out of my blue-tinted daydream. In fact, it was so earsplitting, most of the shoppers actually fell to their knees.

When the fire alarm sounded, a stampede began clamoring for the exit. Anyone carrying a garment dropped it immediately and ran. I wasn't about to leave the sale empty-handed. But then I thought, how would it look if my body was found cradling a blood-soaked designer gown in my arms? "Oh, the irony," people would say, shaking their heads. With that, I took a deep breath, dropped the goods, and fled.

Turns out, the explosion we'd heard was the result of an accident at the technical trade school next door. The blast had blown the façade off the building's stone doorway to be sure, but it was an accident and absolutely no one was hurt.

I returned to the sale the next day, but my dress was a no-show. I guess some other savvy shopper recognized its potential as a sleeveless wedding gown and beat me to the punch. But I did find a dress similar to it (yep, this one had a torn strap, too). A scattering of yellow flowers with pretty green stems beckoned to me like a bright ray of light, and I knew it was meant to be. Or at least that I could make it work. While I wasn't willing to risk my life for the sake of a bargain, paying full price is never an option.

—Maria, 27, Coney Island, New York

SOLUTION 6

Dig for Deals at Yard Sales

We all know one woman's trash is another woman's treasure. Fabulous deals on antiques, jewelry, and vintage clothes await you at yard sales (also known as tag, garage, and stoop sales).

- **Check newspaper classified ads** or community bulletins for where-and-when info.

- **If you're planning to visit several sales** in one day, jot down each address and plan out your route in detail—in fact, that's a perfect task for your husband or boyfriend.

- **Go early** to find the best selections. You may also get better deals toward the end of the sale.

- **When buying dishes or glassware,** beware of any nicks or scratches. Gently run your hand over each piece in case your eyes missed a defect.

- **You usually won't be able try garments on,** so know your measurements (and your kids') and bring along a tape measure.

- **Always bring small bills** and lots of change and don't be afraid to haggle.

Let's Negotiate

Do you know how to haggle? A little good-natured negotiating is often expected and part of the fun. Here's how:

- **Do your research.** *Know how much an item costs elsewhere and point this out to the seller.*

- **Don't risk insulting the seller** *by asking for a huge—and unfair—discount.*

- **Be confident when making your offer.** *If you show any hesitation, you risk losing your bargaining leverage.*

- **Being able to pay in cash** *always sweetens the deal—and lots of sellers will skip the tax if you pay cash. If they don't offer to do this, say, "If I pay cash, can you take off the tax?" Or, if the item is $60, simply say, "If I pay cash, will you take $40?"*

- **If an item is damaged,** *the seller will almost always agree to a discount. Say, "I love this blouse, but there's a pencil mark on it. Is there anything you can do for me about the price?"*

- **Walking away** *can often get you the lowest possible offer, but be prepared to leave empty-handed.*

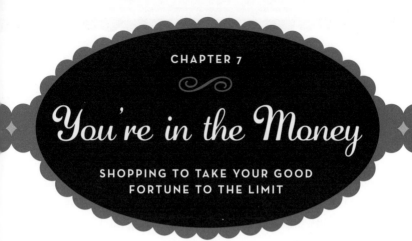

"If I had a million dollars…" Most of the time, this really is wishful thinking, but every once in a while you might get lucky and receive a windfall: a tax refund, inheritance, gambling winnings, Christmas bonus, or even a $100 bill found in the back of a taxicab. Practical friends may attempt to kill your euphoria: "Invest it," they'll say, "or put it into your savings account." Don't succumb to this bourgeois mindset! Every retail therapy devotee knows that you're much better off spending the money on an over-the-top extravagance.

Shop for Fine Jewelry

I don't have anything against costume jewelry, but if you've got the cash, why not spend it on the real deal? Fine jewelry, wrought with precious metals and a glittering rainbow of gems, combines all the intrinsic properties of art, fashion, and earth science into a dazzling creation with the power to take your breath away every time you wear it. Whether you splurge on a piece designed by a master jeweler or troll for more affordable jewels on the internet, fine jewelry is always a smart investment because it's beautiful, wearable, and valuable. Here are some buying tips to keep in mind:

DIAMONDS

Skillfully juggle the Four Cs—the factors that determine the quality of a diamond and its price—and you will get a gem that suits you financially and aesthetically.

● **Cut:** *The way in which a craftsperson carves a rough stone into a glittery gem with perfectly proportioned facets.*

- **Clarity:** *The amount of inclusions, or naturally occurring blemishes, a diamond has. The fewer there are, the better the quality.*

- **Color:** *The best stones look colorless or white.*

- **Carat weight:** *The higher the carat weight, the bigger the stone.*

It's best to upgrade on color and downgrade on clarity. Also, you'll get a better deal if you go a tiny bit smaller than your desired carat weight. Say, a pair of studs with a total carat weight of .97 as opposed to 1.0.

COLORED GEMS

The most prized colored gemstones display spectacular, evenly distributed color and reflect light beautifully. There's nothing wrong with rubies, sapphires, and emeralds, but also consider other fine gems, which tend to display more unusual hues. For example, some tourmalines come in a gorgeous, mermaidy shade of teal; rhodolite garnets are an uncanny shade of magenta.

PEARLS

When buying a strand of pearls, look for:

- **Luster:** *Good pearls glow from within and display a mysterious outer iridescence. Low-luster pearls look opaque.*

- **Surface cleanliness:** *Each pearl should appear smooth and flawless.*

- **Color:** *Pearls come in a variety of "white" shades. Some look creamy or silvery, as opposed to stark white. Other pearls are golden, or have a lovely blush-pink cast.*

- **Size:** *The larger the pearl, the higher the price. Pearls that are 7 to 7.5 mm in diameter (each is about the size of a plump pea) are considered a great value, but the best size is 9 to 10 mm.*

- **Uniformity:** *All of the pearls on the necklace should match each other in terms of size, shape, and color.*

- **Stringing:** *There should be a knot in between each pearl, which prevents scratching and keeps the gems from scattering if the string breaks.*

ATTENTION SHOPPERS

Sales Bitch

I don't care whose handbag you're carrying, or how much cash you just stuffed into it—no one is immune to the haughty, blatantly judgmental gaze of a snooty salesperson. You should never let Suzy Snotface's off-putting vibe thwart your upwardly mobile aspirations, but you'll get better service if you:

- **Look the part.** *If you're shopping at an upscale boutique, dress up a little and wear some makeup.*

- **Exude confidence.** *Stroll into the store with your head held high—you're on a mission!*

- **Ask questions.** *If a salesperson approaches you, don't say you're "just looking." The more interest you show, the more helpful he or she will be.*

- **Play it cool.** *Don't peek at price tags in front of the sales team.*

- **Know your labels.** *Sorry, but pronouncing a designer's name incorrectly is as gauche as it gets.*

- **Know your credit limit.** *Spare yourself the nightmare of having your credit card declined.*

Commission a One-of-a-Kind Dress

Whether it's a party dress or a bespoke suit, the idea of having a garment custom made is so romantic. I remember reading Diana Trilling's essay "A Visit to Camelot" in the *New Yorker* years ago, in which she describes attending a dinner party, held in honor of the 1962 Nobel laureates, at the Kennedy White House. In her account, she shares a story of shopping for a gown to wear to the event, first at a boutique and finally at a New York City dressmaker's atelier, where the garments are "made to order." Here, she manages to snag a sample off-the-rack, a gown of floral-printed moiré taffeta ($250 including alterations!) that she wears to the party with long, white gloves.

Even if you haven't been invited to a black-tie shindig, commissioning a custom-made frock is the ultimate treat. Just knowing that something appropriate for such an occasion hangs in your closet will make you feel like a card-carrying member of the jet set. Joseph Ting, owner of Dynasty Custom Tailors in New York City, gave me the lowdown on this high-fashion indulgence:

1. **Schedule a consultation** with a reputable tailor or dressmaker.

2. **Have a basic idea of the dress you want.** The dressmaker may offer an array of silhouettes to choose from, which you can personalize through your choice of color and fabric, (tweaking the sleeves and hem are standard, too). You can also browse magazines for inspiring dresses, and you should bring these visuals with you to the appointment. If you have access to a pattern that you want replicated, bring that, too.

3. **As for fabric,** you can purchase it yourself or select it with your tailor. A size 6 cocktail dress might require 3 yards.

4. **After you and your tailor have finalized the style and fabric,** your next step will be to schedule your fittings. Expect to have at least three appointments. At the first fitting, your tailor will typically use muslin to draw out the neckline and waistline of the dress. Take this opportunity to discuss changes to ensure that you end up with the dress of your dreams.

• SOLUTION 3 •

Invest in Fine Art

Why spend your windfall on a piece of artwork? "The point of living with art is to experience pleasure," says Angela Di Bello, director of the Agora Gallery in New York City. What retail therapy devotee would want to deny herself of *that*? Here's how to shop for art like a connoisseur:

- **What's your passion:** *Photography? Sculpture? Watercolor? To narrow your search, figure out the medium that most intrigues you. Check out art-mine.com, boundlessgallery.com, biddingtons.com, and hometownartgallery.com. Make arrangements to view a piece in person before buying it.*

- **Establish a budget.** *Some people purchase art strictly to adorn their home or office, while others purchase with appreciation on the brain. If you hope to eventually sell the piece, consider hiring an art dealer. You might also contact auction houses like Christie's or Sotheby's to find out about upcoming auctions.*

- **Only have a few hundred bucks to spare?** *Local art schools and small galleries often carry the work of young, unknown (as yet) artists. Or put your windfall toward a first-rate custom framing job of a poster or print long stashed in a closet.*

ATTENTION SHOPPERS

A Woman's Right to Shop

Every girl who loves to shop would be in big trouble if the government ever tries to introduce a sumptuary law—any law that aims to regulate personal shopping and spending habits as a way to suppress excessive displays of luxury and extravagance. But if it ever happens, let's take this approach:

In Ancient Rome, around 213 B.C., a sumptuary law known as the *lex Oppia* imposed restrictions on the kind of adornment and finery women could purchase and wear in public. Years later, the law was repealed thanks to the efforts of some influential Roman matrons, who led their fellow female citizens in a dramatic protest, and supposedly withheld sex from their husbands. Women who lived in rural areas joined their sisters in the city to take part in the demonstrations, too, and together they crowded the streets, pleading their case to any man who would listen. Many statesmen opposed the repeal of the *lex Oppia*, arguing that without government legislation, women would spend their husbands' money willy-nilly. But other tribunes wisely (wink, wink) defended their women's right to spend money on, and wear, pretty things.

Shop for a Spa Vacation

Remember the original Clairol Herbal Essence shampoo? It was an uncanny shade of emerald-green and the label featured an illustration of a nymph-like woman, her long, blonde hair cascading into a freshwater pool full of flowers and herbs. This is the image that props up my vision of the ultimate spa experience, and were I to come into some cash, I would definitely consider dropping it on a week's worth of sweet-smelling spa treatments to make my skin glow, my hair glisten, and my entire body hum with enervated bliss. Here's how to choose and plan the spa vacation of your dreams.

- **Check out online booking websites** that specialize in spa vacations, like spafinder.com and spachoice.com. You'll be able to browse through a huge database of resorts located around the world to see which ones best suit your desires and budget.

- **Note that there are two types of spas:** a destination spa and a spa resort. The former is usually an all-inclusive experience with specific program guidelines (including meal restrictions) that help you achieve a wellness goal. A spa resort can simply be any hotel with an in-house spa.

- **When choosing a spa,** think about what you want to get out of the experience. Are you looking to improve your lifestyle? Then a resort like Canyon Ranch in Tucson, Arizona, might be a good option, since it offers dozens of treatment programs run by medical doctors and exercise specialists. Some spas offer outdoor adventures like rock-climbing and kayaking, while others are strictly about pampering and indulging you in the most serene surroundings imaginable (think: waterfalls, gardens, and koi ponds).

- **Once you've found a spa** you think you'd like to visit, look closely at its website to be sure its programs, activities, and treatments are what you're looking for. If herbal tea and yoga classes sound like a bore, seek out a spa that encourages you and your girlfriends to yuk it up over margaritas.

- **Schedule your spa treatments** when you make your reservations. Otherwise, you risk not getting the treatments or times you want. Most guests opt for two services a day—say, a massage and facial or a massage and body wrap. Massages should always come before facials, since your head will rest in a face cradle for the duration of the massage. But don't try to do it all. Choose a focus (health and wellness, or ample pampering) and stick with it.

· SOLUTION 5 ·

Hire an Interior Designer

If someone handed me an envelope with a few thousand dollars in it, I would splurge on a curved headboard for the back of my bed. Then I'd have it upholstered in shiny, tufted royal blue or coral satin—so *Valley of the Dolls*! If someone handed me a lot more than a few thousand dollars, I would hire an interior designer to re-do my entire apartment, soup to nuts. If this sounds like your idea of nirvana, too, here's how to get started:

- *Find a pro.* Contact your local design center, or visit the American Society of Interior Designers' website, www.interiors.org.

- *Know what you want.* Do you want one room decorated? The entire house? Tasteful antiques? A heart-shaped waterbed?

- *Set up a consultation.* There's usually a fee for this; find out what it is before you commit. Bring photos or tear sheets that communicate the colors and aesthetics you appreciate.

- *Find out how you'll be charged.* Some pros charge a flat rate for the entire project, while others have an hourly fee. "Cost plus" is another option—the designer purchases the products and services, and sells them to you at cost plus 30 to 50 percent.

Get Your Teeth Professionally Whitened

I know I could have bright-white teeth if I a) gave up Starbucks; b) brushed my teeth compulsively after every meal; and c) devoted time and energy to one of those at-home whitening systems, but I'm too addicted to caffeine and too lazy to deal with anything beyond basic oral hygiene. So the idea of visiting a cosmetic dentist for a megawatt smile makeover has always struck me as a worth-every-penny luxury. If you've come into some unexpected capital, and you also liken gleaming-white teeth to a gorgeous, happy-making accessory you can wear 24/7, skip the D.I.Y. whitening kits and pay a pro to do it properly—most dentists are able to perform whitening procedures in under an hour. Consider:

- ***In-Office Bleaching:*** *Bleaching solutions and gels are applied to the teeth and are activated via light or laser treatment. Most dentists report that results last at least six months.*

- ***Veneers:*** *A thin, porcelain-like laminate is bonded to the front of each tooth. This would be your "couture" option—prices start at $1,000 per tooth!—but, results last at least 5 years.*

"It worked for me!"

ONE SHOPPER'S SUCCESS STORY

On my first trip to Las Vegas, I hit it big at a roulette table: I won almost $1,000 on Number 11. Just hours before, I'd been invited to attend a black-tie dinner and I hadn't packed anything appropriate to wear! So what did I do? I took my winnings and headed straight for the Forum Shops, a fabulous mall adjacent to my hotel, and purchased a new outfit head-to-toe. Here's what I bought:

- **A black silk-faille suit** that I still wear

- **An elegant evening bag**

- **A pair of Giuseppe Zanotti black satin pumps**

- **Victoria's Secret underwear**

- **Black, back-seamed stockings**

The next night at the dinner, a co-worker told everyone how I happened to come by the new ensemble, and the story, as well as the outfit, ended up being the toast of the party. I've never hit Number 11 again, so I know I was destined to win when I did and enjoy that wild shopping spree. I don't regret it for a second.

—Laurie, 41, Miami, Florida

CHAPTER 8

The Blah Factor

SHOPPING TO KILL TIME

Every retail therapy devotee knows that when you have nothing to do, shopping is the most galvanizing activity in existence. There's simply no better way to pass the time—and scare up a little fun for yourself to boot. Heading out to your favorite store may be all it takes to lift you out of your lethargic mood, but there are many other retail therapy techniques to consider if treating a bad case of boredom is your primary goal. Here's how to turn ennui into genuine excitement.

"The Perfect..." Shopping Challenge

When you're really bored and think your usual shopping haunts won't stimulate you, set forth a near-impossible retail challenge for yourself. Here are some pie-in-the-sky quests to consider.

- *The perfect* pair of day-into-evening black pumps

- *A perfectly fitting* pair of jeans

- *The perfect* summer-into-fall, or winter-into-spring outfit

- *The perfect* shade of red lipstick

- *The perfect* "barely there" shade of pink nail polish

- *The perfect* "special occasion" fragrance

- *The perfect* state-of-the-art coffeemaker or espresso machine

- *The perfect* shade of white paint

- *The perfect* CD mix (browse and purchase songs at apple.com/itunes)

- *The perfect* cute-but-not-too-cute cell phone

Check Out a Supermarket

Grocery shopping may not tickle you the way a trip to the mall does—but with a little forethought, a visit to your local grocery store can be educational, sensually satisfying, and weirdly thrilling.

- **Grab three things you have never bought before** but have always been curious about—say, a Lean Cuisine entrée, a jar of rose petal jelly, and a box of Frosted Lucky Charms cereal. Only bring home one of these items (you can flip a coin).

- **Visit the meat department** and, just for kicks, look for the weirdest item they're selling. Quail? Pig's feet? Oxtails?

- **Print out a complicated recipe** and try to hunt down all the ingredients in 10 minutes or less.

- **Pretend you're a social psychologist** and analyze the layout of the supermarket. When you walked in, was your first sight produce and/or fresh flowers? (This is meant to stimulate you and immerse you in an aura of hand-picked freshness.) Are the soups organized in alphabetical order? (Probably not—alphabetized organization tends to decrease sales.)

Browse a Bookstore

Shopping may not be the most intellectually stimulating way to occupy your time—a trip to Marshall's isn't exactly on par with taking in a museum exhibit or going to the opera. However, a retail therapy devotee who wants something fun and intellectually stimulating to do when she's bored has only to head to her local bookstore. There, you can read entire magazines, hunker down with a book of poems, stay abreast of bestsellers, or marvel at beautiful photography in a giant coffee table book. No matter what your interests—cooking, crafting, crossword puzzles, erotica, sports, history, finance—you'll always find a book you can lose yourself in for a few minutes or a few hours.

Shopping the children's section of a bookstore is fun, too. Gorgeously illustrated volumes of classic fairy stories like *The Snow Queen* or *Cinderella* make excellent gifts for "friends who have everything." And you'll love rediscovering titles from childhood you've long since forgotten.

For passionate devotees of retail therapy, your bookstore is also well-stocked with shopping-related tomes, from "chick lit" to how-to manuals and guide books. And don't forget *Lucky* magazine!

Double Happiness

Q. *Shopping is fine for some, but I like to self-medicate the old-fashioned way. Where are the best places to shop when you're under the influence?*

A. The candy, snack, and frozen food sections of your local 7-Eleven is the obvious choice (please make sure someone drives you!); it hardly bears mentioning if you've ever experienced the munchies. Any kind of outdoor market, especially a flea market or crafts fair, is also ripe with opportunities to see and buy intriguing things, and talking with the artists and designers who are selling their wares often makes for trippy conversation. Stores that sell candles are also irresistible to the inebriated shopper—they're so colorful and fragrant, and possess the most tantalizing names: Pineapple Cilantro, Wasabi Mint, Vanilla Honeyblossom...

Just don't go anywhere too hoity-toity, no matter how hilarious this idea seems at the time. The last thing you need when you're a little out of it is a disapproving gaze from a salesperson (or a threatening one from a security guard!). And if you're prone to paranoia, this kind of environment is a danger zone.

Home Improvement to the Rescue

If you're anything like me, you like shopping for clothes and cosmetics best, but when you're bored, why not shop outside your comfort zone? For me this would definitely be a home-improvement center like Home Depot or Lowe's. I figure I can sample perfume and try on pairs of earrings any day of the week, but how often do I get to browse through books of wallpaper?

In grade school, they used to have us create collages with wallpaper scraps, cutting and pasting snips of it onto construction paper in elaborate, fancy-free configurations. As an adult, flipping through a book of wallpaper taps into a similarly imaginative part of the psyche. You'll find yourself daydreaming about how to decorate rooms you don't even own: a crimson Chinoiserie pattern displaying pagodas and periwinkle-blue lotus blossoms for a dining room, Peter Rabbit prints for a nursery, lavender toile for a guest room...

The paint department of a home-improvement store will also fan the flame of your wildest interior design fantasies. There's something deeply exhilarating about all of those paint chips, both the sight of so many different colors and the evocative names: Pink Corsage, Night Flower, Golden Kiwi, Starched Apron... Pocket as many paint chips as you like. Use them to contemplate how you might freshen up your walls, of course, but also consider using them in scrapbooking projects or as gift tags for presents.

• SOLUTION 5 •

Kill Time Online

Everyone knows you're most likely to encounter feelings of boredom in the workplace. But the retail therapy devotee is rarely bored at work because she knows that the internet is bursting with opportunities to browse and buy, especially when it comes to scoring deals and tracking down hard-to-find items.

Of course, technically, you don't have to be "bored" to shop online. Sometimes procrastination is the motivation, in which case the sites you visit need to be engrossing and pleasurable enough to keep you from completing whatever task you're trying to avoid. I'm all too familiar with my favorite shopping sites, and I talked to other retail therapy devotees to find out theirs. Bookmark these:

abebooks.com   *delight.com*

adiamondisforever.com   *drugstore.com*

amazon.com   *ebay.com*

bidz.com   *eluxury.com*

bluefly.com   *garnethill.com*

cb2.com   *girlshop.com*

dailycandy.com   *iomoi.com*

jcrew.com

laredoute.com

metmuseum.org

moma.org

poshgirlvintage.com

sephora.com

shopnbc.com

silverjewelryclub.com

smallflower.com

smartbargains.com

snappy-turtle.com

splendora.com

tias.com

vivre.com

yoox.com

zappos.com

The Comatose Cashier

Think you're bored? Consider the listless guy or girl working the checkout counter where you're shopping—talk about world-weary! Really posh stores rarely make you wait on line at a register. It's the chain stores that always seem to have the slowest lines, and the pokiest sales staff. Unfortunately, both can frustrate you to the point of undoing the pleasurable effects of retail therapy. So stay calm—there are ways to kill time while you wait. You can:

- **Break out a book** or magazine.

- **Send a text message** to a friend you haven't reached out to in a while.

- **Eavesdrop** on conversations around you.

- **Play a game** on your cell phone.

- **Observe** how your fellow shoppers are dressed.

- **Observe** what your fellow shoppers are buying—commit the goods you'd like to own to memory.

- **Re-apply** your makeup.

- **Take out a notebook** and compose (or edit) a to-do list.

- **Plan your exit strategy** (especially helpful in malls).

• SOLUTION 6 •

Turn on the TV

The ability to entertain yourself is quite a skill—I grew up an only child in a house in which TV time was regulated, Barbie dolls were not permitted (blocks and Star Wars figures were allowed, though), and book reading was everyone's idea of fun. But the day I got in trouble and was banished to my room with a firm "No TV tonight!," I didn't pick up my copy of *Anne of Green Gables*. No, I built myself a TV set with the blocks—complete with a paper "screen" displaying Magic Marker characters and sets.

More recently, I've dated guys who don't have televisions, and they reveal this to me grandly, as if to impress me with their disdain for "mindless" activity and consumer culture. But no one will ever convince me that TV is the enemy—and you shouldn't let anyone convince you, either. Especially when there are so many programs designed to push your buttons. Obviously, there are the shopping channels, QVC and ShopNBC, which tempt you to take your spendorphins to the next level with shows that sell jewelry, scrapbooking materials, cookware, and cosmetics. But there are a host of other boredom-slaying offerings you should sample, as well, from *Antiques Road Show* to *Queer Eye for the Straight Guy* to anything on the Style Network.

"It worked for me!"

ONE SHOPPER'S SUCCESS STORY

I spend a good part of my day shopping—either online or just watching the shopping channels on TV. It's 11 A.M. and I'm shopping a sale at talbots.com when I should be working; it's 1:30 and I'm checking out the jewelry clearance items on overstock.com when I should be working; it's 6 P.M. and I'm watching Now You're Cooking on QVC as I eat my dinner; it's 10 P.M. and I'm flipping back and forth between 10,000 Carat Celebration on ShopNBC and Law & Order reruns. People think I'm this deranged shopaholic, and maybe I am, but what my critics fail to recognize is that I have a fantastic time doing it. I have other interests. I'd much rather go to the opera or see a movie with a friend than shop; however, I'm quite passionate about my "hobby," and if you've nothing better to do, shopping is a great way to pass the time. The thrill of the hunt is so stimulating, and when you shop the internet, catalogs, and TV as I do, you fall in love with the buzz of expecting your packages. Come home to one or two of these and you're instantly over the moon.

I remember the first piece I bought from QVC: a $15 silver herringbone chain. I think a lot of people start with silver, as it's so affordable. It was beautiful—and the rest is history! I also remember my first purchase from ValueVision (now ShopNBC). They just appeared on my TV one day and I instantly started "cheating" on QVC because the goods seemed much more high-end. The first thing I ordered was a heavy 14K gold omega-link chain—a steal at just under $12 a gram. The total was $400 but they offered "Valuepay": you're billed in three to four staggered installments (interest free!) so that the entire sum doesn't show up on your credit card all at once.

I didn't have the internet until 1998. I started slowly, because I was concerned about putting my credit card info on the net. But I got over that. My first internet purchase was a Dell computer (a colleague walked me through the purchase at work). Right now I think the internet is more entertaining. You're not restricted to what's showing on TV—sometimes they slog just a few things for an entire hour and it can get boring. To date, I have purchased all kinds of things online—appliances, cookware, jewelry, watches, clothes, shoes, furniture, collectibles, purses, and specialty food items. And it's always a good time.

—Catherine, 54, Lynn, Massachusetts

CHAPTER 9

Spread the Love

RETAIL STRATEGIES FOR THE BENEVOLENT NARCISSIST

Self-centered. Self-absorbed. Vain. If I had a nickel for every time I've reproached myself for embodying what these words convey, I'd have a huge chunk of change. Dwelling on it, though, can undo the positive effects of retail therapy. Instead, I've discovered that being consistently kind and generous—being what I call a "benevolent narcissist"—alleviates the emotional distress that comes with overindulgence, overspending, and other forms of buyer's remorse. Sometimes a halo is the only accessory a girl really needs to get through the day.

• SOLUTION 1 •

Shop for a Charity

The easiest way to curb those feelings of excessive self-indulgence? Give to charity. But there are so many worthy causes—which ones should you support? Here's how to sift through the sea of nonprofits to find one that speaks to your heart.

- ● *For overviews of national charities,* visit give.org, the website of the BBB Wise Giving Alliance, a partnership between the National Charities Information Bureau and the Council of Better Business Bureaus. Charitynavigator.com, a nonprofit group that provides unbiased evaluations of more than 5,000 American charities, is another great resource.

- ● *To gather additional information* about a charity before you make a contribution, ask to see its annual reports. The IRS or your state attorney general's office should have info on file, too.

- ● *Be sure your charity's mission statement* is clearly defined and that its short- and long-term goals are quantifiable. It's difficult to know if a charity is truly making a difference if its objectives are vague.

- **Find out how much progress** the charity has made toward achieving its goals. You should only support charities that are serious in their commitments and have results to back them up.

- **Support the underdogs.** The big, heavily publicized charities get lots of donations, but there are a lot of little charities, often with very specific, small-scale goals that deserve your attention. For example, one year during the holiday season, instead of giving to the Humane Society, I donated to a "rabbit rescue" in Connecticut (a one-woman organization that places abandoned or unwanted rabbits in good homes). While I love cats and dogs, I felt that lots of people would remember these animals at holiday time, and that very few people would be thinking about those poor little bunnies!

• SOLUTION 2 •

Shop for Friends and Family

Shopping for someone other than yourself is one of most healing forms of retail therapy. First of all, while it may be difficult to rationalize spending money on "gifts" for yourself, buying gifts for someone else gives you carte blanche to spend whatever you like. Having someone else to shop for automatically broadens the selection of goods to choose from and increases the amount of territory you get to pillage in any given store. And finding "just the thing" for someone, whether it's a friend, coworker, or relative, is extremely gratifying. Things to keep in mind:

● **Give spontaneously!** *Buy someone a present "just because"— an upcoming special occasion isn't required. But if having a "good reason" is essential to your m.o., keep in mind that one can buy holiday gifts for people at any time of year.*

● **Kids rock.** *Shopping for children is always a blast, whether you're picking out toys, treats, or cute little outfits.*

- **_Think ahead._** _For best results, keep a list of friends' and relatives' sizes, china patterns, mattress sizes, favorite colors, et cetera in your purse. If you spot something you think he/she might like, you can cross-reference it with this dossier._

- **_Provide a service._** _We all have friends, family members, and lovers who don't like to shop, don't know how to shop, or don't have time to shop. No one can call you selfish or self-absorbed if you're putting your valuable skills to use on someone else's behalf. Be the official "personal shopper" of your circle—ask people close to you to tell you if there's something specific they're looking for with the understanding that you'll find it, buy it, and expect to be reimbursed. The next time you go out shopping for yourself, you'll also be on the lookout for your "clients." Make sure you have your cell phone handy in case you need to run something by them._

Happy Holidays

Q. *Is it okay to buy things for myself when I'm supposed to be holiday shopping for friends and family?*

A. Don't be silly, of course it's okay! The holidays are a crazy time of year. Most people vacillate between sparkly eyed feelings of warmth and excitement, and teary-eyed descents into loneliness, bitterness, and self-recrimination. Retail therapy is what will shepherd you out of the doldrums—straying from your holiday shopping list to purchase yourself the occasional pick-me-up might be the only thing that keeps you sane. And there are so many wonderful holiday treats to indulge in—decorations, party outfits, glittery decorations, champagne, ribbons, gift wrap, boxes of chocolate, holiday CDs, and so on. Think of it this way: You're not being selfish—you're being festive!

SOLUTION 3

What Goes Around, Comes Around

A truly benevolent narcissist wants to help save the world...but she also wants a little something for herself (something cuter than a tax write-off, that is). Your best bets:

- **UNICEF (unicefusa.org):** *This nonprofit, dedicated to improving the lives of disadvantaged children around the world, was founded by the United Nations. It has corporate partnerships with retailers like IKEA, which sells UNICEF greeting cards year-round. In their catalog, you'll find unusual handmade objets and accessories for yourself, as well adorable toys and games for kids.*

- **Goods That Give (goodsthatgive.com):** *This online shop sells earth-friendly gift items and donates a portion of the proceeds to community-based nonprofits. Products include: gourmet foods, home accessories, jewelry, and beauty products—such as a collection of citrus-scented soaps from the Enterprising Kitchen, a Chicago-based nonprofit that provides employment training to low-income women.*

- **Charity e-malls:** *There are a number of websites that let you shop well-known merchants and donate a portion of the sale to one of your favorite charities. Here are three to consider:*

    Buyforcharity.com: Up to 35 percent of your purchase will go to your charity.

    Igive.com: You can choose from thousands of charities or add one to the list.

    givingworks.ebay.com: If, like me, you're an eBay junkie, bookmark this genius website, which allows you to search for items sold by sellers who will donate a portion of your sale to a charity they've partnered with.

Everything Must Go

It sure feels great to clean out your closet and give your old clothes and accessories to the needy, but excess is lurking in other areas of your life, too. Here's a "most wanted" list of items you can donate, and some causes they support:

- **Cell phones:** *Enter your zip code at americancellphonedrive.org to find the nearest drop-off location.*

- **Books:** *Donate books to your local library or to a public school that needs them.*

- **Furniture and household appliances:** *The good old Goodwill and other charity thrift stores accepts these items. Call ahead.*

- **Hair:** *Help children suffering from long-term medical hair loss by donating your hair to locksoflove.org.*

- **Old linens, blankets, and towels:** *Local animal shelters will welcome these.*

- **Computers:** *World Computer Exchange (worldcomputerex-change.org) will take your old machine off your hands and refurbish it for poor children in developing countries.*

SOLUTION 4

Donate Clothing

Somewhere in your closet, there's a garbage bag overflowing with clothes you plan to donate to Goodwill or the Salvation Army. When it comes to ridding your closet of undesirable items, these organizations are the retail therapy devotee's default charities, but there are lots of other groups that will appreciate your hand-me-downs—especially when (admit it) so many of your clothes and accessories are barely worn and designer quality. Consider:

● **Dress for Success (dressforsuccess.org):** *Its mission is to aid low-income women in entering the workforce and retaining their jobs. The nonprofit organization relies on financial contributions as well as donations of business attire for its clients. Check its website for a drop-off location near you.*

● **The Women's Alliance (thewomensalliance.org):** *Another national organization, made up of independent, community-based members, which offers career training for women in need and provides them with professional attire. Drop-off locations are listed online.*

- **The Glass Slipper Project (glassslipperproject.org):** This Chicago-based grassroots organization accepts donations of formal dresses, shoes, purses, jewelry, and unopened cosmetics for low-income high school students (juniors and seniors only) in need of prom dresses and accessories. "Boutique sales" at the organization's headquarters are held annually. Its website lists similar prom-dress programs throughout the U.S. and Canada.

- **Domestic-abuse shelters:** Contact your local police department, church or synagogue, or women's advocacy groups for information about how to make donations to domestic-abuse shelters. For the safety of the clients, you won't find these addresses posted publicly.

"It worked for me!"

ONE SHOPPER'S SUCCESS STORY

When I learned that Hurricane Katrina had touched down in New Orleans, I knew I had to do something. Two very special friends in New Orleans managed to call me, and broke my heart with stories about people losing everything they had. It was such a desperate situation—many people didn't even have clothes—so organizing a clothing drive was my immediate response.

In New York City, many of us have so much and all I could think about was how great it would be if everyone I knew personally, or by association, went into their closets to pick out clothes to donate. My New Orleans' friends gave me a few direct addresses to ship boxes of clothes to, and with that, I jumped in and got started. At Goldstein Communications, the public relations/event-planning agency where I work, we have a huge database containing the e-mail addresses of all our media and industry contacts. So I created a letter asking for contributions to our clothing drive and everyone in the office started e-mailing everyone we knew to get the word out. I'm sure we reached out to 10 or 20 thousand people.

Our office served as a drop-off center and instead of sending to the larger organizations, we mailed clothes directly to vic-

tims and local churches. We received bags and bags of cloth-ing—clean, dirty, smelly, brand-new...we accepted it all. Two coworkers and I sorted through the clothing so that we could send the sizes needed. FedEx gave us a discount on the boxes we used, and we charged the shipping to our company's credit card. We sent a steady supply of clothes for about a month.

Looking back, it would have been helpful to have had a plethora of free boxes and chargeable shipping accounts, and if I could do it over, I would have waited another week before send-ing out our donations; some of the boxes we sent kept bouncing back to us because the victims of the Hurricane had to keep mov-ing. But I'm extremely proud of what I accomplished. I am a pub-licist and an event planner, but anyone can jump in and help when disaster hits. When you give selflessly to people in need, you fill up with joy and feel so good. If you're interested in get-ting involved with a charity, go for it. Find an organization that interests you and give your time. Even if you don't have money or items to give, every organization needs a helping hand.

—Rachel P. Goldstein, Vice President, Entertainment & Special Events, Goldstein Communications, Ltd., New York City

• SOLUTION 5 •

Cash In

As a benevolent narcissist, you're entitled to act in your own self-interest from time to time. This scenario is probably very familiar: While cleaning out your closet, you stumble on a pair of yellow Marni flats you haven't worn in…actually you've never worn them, have you? You're about to toss them into the Good Will pile, but then you remember how much you spent on them—$129.99, the Century 21 price tag is still on them! You know you have to get rid of them to make room for the newest members of your shoe collection, but the idea of all that money going to waste is making you sick to your stomach. Maybe there's something in your closet you can return, as punishment for the careless spending that got you into this situation…?

Come on, there are better ways to deal with buyer's remorse! Consider these "when life gives you lemons…" alternatives:

1 ***Sell your unwanted item in the classifieds*** *section of your local newspaper or create a free listing in the "for sale" section of craigslist.org.*

2 ***Sell your unwanted item to a used clothing store—****great for instant gratification, but don't expect a lot of cash. One of the*

used clothing boutiques in my neighborhood tried to offer me a mere $5 for a pair of Miu Miu galoshes.

3 **Sell your unwanted item to a local consignment store.** * Or better yet, put them up for auction on eBay. You can even have an authorized third-party "trading assistant" take care of the selling and shipping logistics for you, with a commission per each item sold.

4 **Give your unwanted item to a friend,** preferably one who rarely buys herself anything nice, or can't afford to do so. Cash is great, but it also feels really, really good to see someone else enjoy what you couldn't.

***Note:** Most consignment stores donate unsold items to charity, so even if you don't get any cash back, someone else stands to benefit in the end. If you're feeling guilty about wanting to put a little bit of cash back into your wallet, hock your stuff through MissionFish (missionfish.org), which allows eBay sellers to donate portions of each sale to the charity of their choice.

Index

Acknowledgments

I would like to thank all of the friends and colleagues who shared their wonderful shopping stories and insights with me, whether in the form of a written "testimonial," a spur-of-the-moment brainstorming session over glasses of wine, or by replying to one of my desperate e-mails lickety-split. I would also like to thank Sarah Scheffel, my editor at Quirk Packaging, for helping me hash out a structure for this book, which made the process of writing it much easier (and prevented me from taking too many retail therapy breaks). I am especially grateful to Rebecca Federman at the New York Public Library for generously contributing her time and expertise to this project and never laughing at the nature of my zany requests for information. Finally, I would like to express my gratitude to Valerie Berrios, who contributed her phenomenal, note-perfect research and reporting skills; Lynne Yeamans, whose design work is so stylish; and Robin Zingone, for her adorable illustrations.